The Accidental Sailor

Rod Heikell

taniwha press uk

Published by the Taniwha Press UK

All rights reserved. No part of this publication may be reproduced, transmitted or used in any form by any means - graphic, electronic or mechanical, including photocopying, recording, taping or information storage and retrieval systems or otherwise - without the prior permission of the Publishers.

© Rod Heikell 2013. Rod Heikell has asserted his right under the Copyright, Designs and Patents Act 1988 to be identified as the author of this work.

British Library Cataloguing in Publication Data
Heikell, Rod

Title   The Accidental Sailor
Type   Non fiction. Sailing. Voyages. Mediterranean
1st edition 2013

ISBN 978-0-9575849-0-7

Printed and bound in the UK by Biddles, part of the MPG Printgroup, Bodmin and King's Lynn

Grateful thanks to Lu who proofed and helped me on the way with this book. Special thanks to Elinor Cole who pushed and prodded the book into shape for the printers and designed the cover. Willie Wilson and Ian Rippington at Imrays helped out in so many ways – my thanks.

The Accidental Sailor

The cabin of a small yacht is a truly wonderful thing, not only will it shelter you from a tempest, but from the other troubles in life it is a safe retreat.
L Francis Herreshoff

Preface

These two accounts of small boat voyages to the Mediterranean are what I would describe as plucky little voyages rather than big brave expeditions. This is not Tilman voyaging to South America to climb little known peaks or David Lewis sailing *Ice Bird* down to Antarctica. These voyages are altogether more modest affairs in the 20 foot *Roulette* through and around France to Greece and in *Rozinante*, a Mirror Offshore 18, down the Danube behind the Iron Curtain and on through the Black Sea to Aegean Turkey.

In 1976-77 I sailed the 20 foot *Roulette*, an old hard chine plywood boat with a dodgy engine and little else down to Greece. No electrics, a steering compass, a few charts, cotton sails and a certain naivety about wind, weather and sea. *Roulette* sailed to St Malo and then through the Britanny Canals to the Bay of Biscay where we coast-hopped down to Bordeaux. The Garonne Canal and Canal du Midi provide a short-cut to the Mediterranean coast of France and a lot of sight-seeing along the way. From here *Roulette* crossed to Corsica, Italy and finally to Greece.

The second voyage in 1987 was in *Rozinante*, a Mirror Offshore 18, that like *Roulette* was also minimally equipped. The voyage down the Danube started in Regensburg in Germany and continued on downstream through the eastern bloc to Constanta on the Black Sea. Being unable to get fuel in Romania the 200 mile passage to Istanbul took four days. After a breather in Istanbul we sailed *Rozinante* on through the Marmara Sea to the Aegean and down to Bodrum on the Turkish coast. This voyage was made before the Iron Curtain tore and the former satellites of the USSR broke free from their communist masters.

My sort of cruising is poking around and gunk-holing around the coast and islands of a country. On ocean passages I don't want to arrive in one place and stay there until the next long passage. The joy of making landfall is to explore the country, pottering around harbours and anchorages and seeing what is going on ashore before retiring to the shelter and comfort of your little ship. One thing I am sure of is that passages, however short, somehow augment the senses. Food tastes better. A cup of tea after a blow is the best tea ever. A glass of red, however humble, is nectar from the gods. Laughter and good company are heightened experiences over the land-based equivalent where conversations seem to be endless recitations about mortgages and the new kitchen. I know that those endorphins in my brain somehow, don't ask me how, work overtime to heighten experiences when voyaging in small ships on the sea.

When recalling the first voyage I discovered, in the jumble of files and papers here in my office, *Roulette's* log from the Loire onwards. The previous log from Yarmouth had gone missing. Like this later log it was probably a little notebook affair that has been ruled up for the entries. It is stained and illegible in places from seawater and the pencil entries have faded though most are still just legible. There are old black and white photos as well, taken with my old Pentax Spotmatic, though there are many that have gone missing. At least this log has kept me honest though lots of the events remain seared in my brain anyway. Part of this account had been written a few years ago and until some friends encouraged me to 'get on with it', it had languished in a near forgotten file on the computer. Most of it was written over 2012–2013.

For the Danube voyage I still have lots of notebooks from the two trips down the river and onwards. The core of the Danube account is from an appendix in my *The Danube: A River Guide*, though much fleshed out from the notebooks.

So what happened on the way to the Mediterranean? I was 27 in 1976 when we set off from England, sure that this little voyage was to be an interstice before I returned to New Zealand and some 'proper job'. You could call it escaping. I prefer to think of it as something of a pilgrimage, though the object of the pilgrimage is obscure. Something happened on this voyage so that bit by bit I fell in love with this life and voyaging to distant places. Some 37 years have gone by now and I'm still on the water. I've taken Cavafy's message in his poem *Ithaca* to heart.

Hope the voyage is a long one.
May there be many a summer morning when,
with what pleasure, what joy,
you come into harbours seen for the first time

Rod Heikell   2013

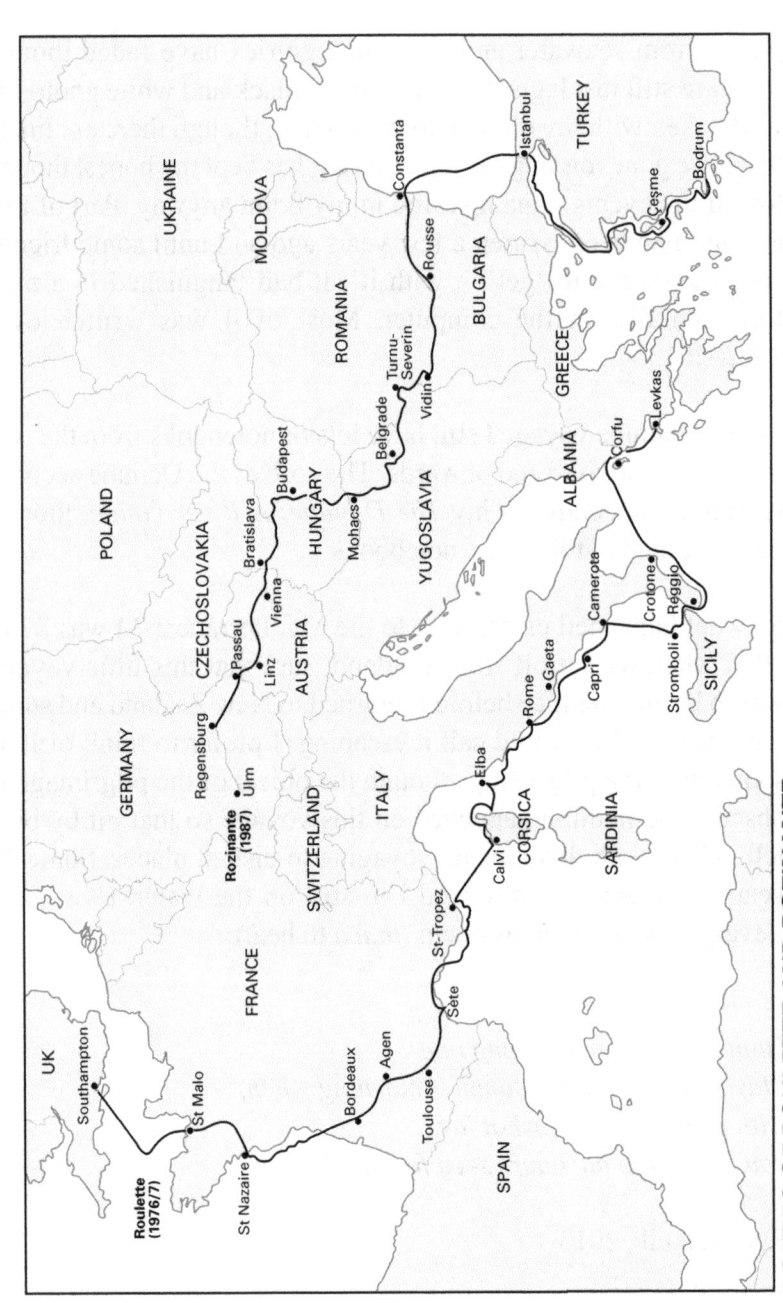

ROUTES OF ROULETTE AND ROZINANTE

Contents

I Roulette *1*
1 The Itch *7*
2 Roulette *13*
3 The Channel *21*
4 Through the Britany Canals *27*
5 Biscay *31*
6 Through the canals to the Mediterranean *39*
7 Mediterranean France *45*
8 Corsica *56*
9 Italy *63*
10 The Ionian *83*
11 Greece *90*
12 Coda *100*

II Rozinante *105*
1 1985 On foot down the Danube *106*
2 1987 Rozinante *113*
3 Germany *118*
4 Austria *125*
5 Czechoslovakia *132*
6 Hungary *145*
7 Yugoslavia *152*
8 Bulgaria *162*
9 Romania *168*
10 The Black Sea *179*
11 Turkey *184*
12 Coda *192*

I Roulette

1976–77

A tale of a small boat voyage to the Mediterranean via the French Canals and the Bay of Biscay to the south of France and on to Corsica, Italy and Greece.

hark, now hear the sailors cry,
smell the sea, and feel the sky
let your soul & spirit fly, into the mystic...
Van Morrison

Who is staring at the sea is already sailing a little.
Paul Carvel

August 1976   Yarmouth to St Malo

It wasn't meant to work out this way. *Roulette* was on her first offshore passage and lots of things weren't going right. Here we were rattling along at 4 knots or so, and 4 knots seemed like a good speed in the 20 foot *Roulette*, somewhere in the English Channel and I wasn't sure exactly where. Our navigation was by dead reckoning using the tidal flow charts in *Reeds Nautical Almanac* to plot vectors on the chart of where the tide pushed or pulled the boat. Using our heading from the steering compass and an estimation of our speed and the application of the tidal vectors, we should know where we are.

After two days in the channel it clearly wasn't working and I was getting worried that none of the lights off the Cherbourg Peninsula and the Channel Islands had flashed over the far horizon and no bits of land had come into view. At the speeds we had been doing, around 3-4 knots most of the time and our direction heading southwest, we should have seen something.

Here we were at the beginning of a grand adventure to sail down to the Mediterranean and somehow we had got lost on the first leg. I was more dulled by the realization that things were going wrong than terrified. None of this was helped by the state of sheer helplessness I had been in earlier.

I had not been feeling great. Or, to put it more brutally, I was seasick and lying down below wishing I was somewhere else. I was disgusted at my apathy and so was Bridget. I lay like a bit of washed-out flotsam on the cabin sole while Bridget steered. Eventually I hear Bridget calling down to me from the cockpit.

Rod, you have to come up and steer. I've been here for 6 hours.

1 Roulette

The words washed over me.

Rod, you have to come up, I can't keep on doing this.

There was a sense of panic in her voice now, not surprising as we were somewhere in the Channel with a pathetic wreck of a man lying on the cabin sole.

Rod, come up here now.

Bridget was exhausted. I pulled myself into the cockpit, retched a few times over the side, and then was miraculously restored. Well if not restored, at least steering, watching the grid bearing compass and the sea and getting on with it. Sort of. I blamed the lamb curry on the first night out and ever since I have had a superstitious fear of eating lamb curry on the first night of a passage. Really I knew that I needed to find some sort of steel inside to pursue this adventure.

Since that time I have never been laid low by seasickness. I've felt nauseous. I've even retched over the side a few times. But I've always taken my watch and been in charge of the boat. What this episode did was give me an empathy with anyone who does succumb to seasickness. It surprises me how many souls do go sailing in the knowledge that they will be seasick and yet such is their passion for sailing, they bravely take it on the nose and keep at it until the seasickness evaporates.

One friend who has a circumnavigation under his belt used to get seasick for the first two or three days of a passage. His advice was to eat canned pineapple – 'tastes as good on the way up as it does on the way down'. Others try every remedy going from natural remedies like ginger to motion sickness pills like

Dramamine, an antihistamine, and Scopolamine, which is used for problems with your balance, just so they can keep sailing. For me fresh air and a more relaxed attitude to setting off on passage works – at least so far.

In the late afternoon the wind increased to around Force 5-6, though still in a favourable direction and *Roulette* bucketed along. The seas were up now and I marvelled at how the tucked in stern lifted to the waves with just the occasional splash into the cockpit. We didn't want any more than the occasional splash as the cockpit was not self draining. We have to see land soon, I thought, and then I saw a French frigate bearing down on us. It hove-to near us with the matelots lined up along the rail, all dressed up with bright red lifejackets on, looking down on *Roulette*. None of them looked comfortable as the frigate wallowed in the swell. I realised now we must look tiny in this sea alongside the frigate. We got the sails down and waved to the crew. One of them had an 8mm camera and was filming us so there must be an old reel of 8mm film somewhere with *Roulette* bobbing up and down in the swell.

One of the officers came out with a megaphone and asked if we were all right.

We are OK.
Are you sure? Do you need anything?
No we don't need anything.
I will report you to Lloyds.
Can you give us a position?
Hold on one minute.

He went inside and then came out and read out the position to us.
Are you sure you don't need anything?
No, we will be all right.

I Roulette

I'm pretty sure there was a quaver in my voice as I replied and the frigate steamed off to the west.

The position we were given put us in the western approaches to the Channel and at least 30 degrees off course. How could that be? We were headed for America not St Malo. I mulled it over for a bit after the frigate had steamed off into the evening gloom and suddenly it hit me. My lovely new mild steel tiller bracket was about 10 inches from the compass and was causing it to deviate by 30 degrees. I had installed the steel tiller bracket after plotting the deviation card in the Solent and after navigating around the Solent when it had worked just fine. I moved the compass and its bracket to the forward end of the cockpit and hoped that solved the problem. It was now on the outside of the bridge deck locker so I went through the locker removing anything I thought might interfere with the compass. With the position the French navy had given us we were now hopefully heading more or less in the right direction for St Malo.

We sailed through the night and then the wind died and the fog came down. We drifted around aimlessly with the tide and I tried to get the engine going to no avail. In the soupy fog there was no sound except the occasional plop of a wavelet on the hull. The visibility was down to a couple of hundred yards. As we drifted around I thought we must be somewhere near Plateau des Roches Douvres some 25 miles west of Jersey in the Channel Islands. Slowly the fog was burned off by the sun and as it cleared out of the mist a huge lighthouse and three jagged pinnacles of rock poking up out of the sea emerged with green water sluicing around the shallow rocky ledge they stand on. Yep. We were close to Roches Douvres. Problem was just a bit too close.

It's easy to be flippant about the situation afterwards. At the time we both thought we were going to die. Or at least be in a very bad place, probably cold, drifting around helplessly in the dinghy, another statistic in the 'small yacht lost in the Channel' report somewhere in some coastguard file. It was the sheer incomprehensibility of it all. Almost as if it was happening to someone else.

I tried the engine again whirling the starter handle on the flywheel around and around. Nothing. No way that Stuart Turner was going to co-operate when it was an emergency. I yelled at Bridget to pump up the dinghy and launch it with the panic bag in it while I kept trying to start the engine. With the inflatable dinghy tied alongside with water and the panic bag in it the tide sucked us onto the rocks.

There was no pretence of calm now. We both thought this was it and that in a few minutes we would be floating around the channel in the dinghy. We watched in horror as the tide picked *Roulette* up and whooshed us towards the rocks and green breaking water. Shit, shit, shit. And we watched still with stunned incomprehensibility as *Roulette* was sluiced between the rocky pinnacles and spat out the other side. Not even a bump. And not a word between the two of us. Somehow *Roulette's* minimal three foot draught had missed the rocks with the tide sucking us through the deeper channels between the rocks where it ran fastest. We recovered the grab bag and deflated the dinghy in silence, amazed we were still afloat and not holed on Roches Douvres.

We were still alive and all we had to do somehow was to find St Malo.

1 The Itch

In 1975 I had £800 and I wanted to sail down to the Mediterranean. It was a year after I had arrived in England and most things in my life seemed to have imploded. Sitting in Woburn Sands in deepest Buckinghamshire, about as far from the sea as you can get in England, an irrational and anarchic impulse had taken hold of my brain and I had become tunnel-vision man. Sailing. Boats. Sea. Navigation. Voyaging somewhere else other than a Britain clothed in grey skies and 25% inflation. I was on a learning curve that exploded off the graph and I needed to satisfy this sailing itch.

I have no idea how it happened. I was supposed to be finishing a thesis on the history of science. Like a naughty child at school I kept castigating myself for sneaking forbidden reading matter into the classroom. Everyone was there. The 'greats' of sailing, the Hiscocks and *Cruising Under Sail*, Sterling Hayden and *Wanderer*, Robin Knox-Johnson's *A World of My Own* and the Smeeton's *Once is Enough*. I read other lesser known authors as well, Donald Riddler's *Erik the Red*, an account of building and sailing a 27ft home-made boat on a £250 budget. And Stanley and Colin Smith's voyage across the Atlantic on *Nova Espero*, a 20ft yawl.

Somehow these latter accounts of small boat voyages described a possibility on my £800 budget. The other accounts all featured boats, beautiful long-keeled beauties like the Hiscock's *Wanderer* and the Smeeton's 46-foot *Tzu Hang,* that seemed so very far away from what I could afford. Robin Knox-Johnson was right out of the picture as some sort of alien who could survive ten and a half months on his own and bring *Suhali* safely back after sailing single-handed around the world. That was out of my league.

I found an old National Geographic that featured the voyage of *Half Safe*, an American amphibious jeep from W.W.II that crossed the Atlantic. Australian Ben Carlin was at a loose end after the war and for whatever reasons, and they are obscure, he embarked upon a scheme to buy a war-surplus amphibious jeep and modify it with extra fuel tanks and weather-proofing and cross from Halifax in Nova Scotia to the Azores. After several attempts and a lot more mods to the jeep, including a towed fuel tank, Carlin arrived in Flores in the Azores after a 32 day trip. From here he motored to Madeira and then across to Morocco. Later he continued on across the Indian Ocean and Pacific to arrive back in Anchorage in the USA. It cost Carlin his marriage and not a few acrimonious fights with various crew members. By all accounts Carlin was a man with a dedicated tunnel-vision for the project and a bitter sarcasm with which he flayed all around him, but he achieved the near impossible feat of a circumnavigation in his amphibious jeep.

In the literature of small boat voyages there was plenty out there to inspire a more modest voyage. *Nova Espero* had crossed the Atlantic twice, the first time without a cabin and just the upturned dinghy for shelter. Patrick Ellam had sailed the Atlantic in *Sopranino*, a beautiful Laurent Giles sloop just under 20 foot long. John Guzzwell had the Laurent Giles designed *Trekka*, a 22 footer, to sail around the world. But it was to the third voyage of *Nova Espero* with Charles Violet at the helm that interested me. *Nova Espero* was just 20ft long and had twice crossed the Atlantic.

When Violet took it down to the Mediterranean it had a fair few miles under it's keel. If Violet could do it in a 20 footer I felt sure that there was a possibility I could. And Violet had done it on a small budget.

I Roulette

...I wanted to start voyaging again, wandering on the water for choice, because there is no better way of reaching distant places than by voyages in a small boat. (Solitary Voyage Charles Violet)

With *Nova Espero* and *Erik the Red* in mind, I devoured yachting magazines and poured over the classified columns. The stumbling block was that I really had little experience with boats and the sea.

Donald Riddler had built *Erik the Red* in his parents garden using old floorboards and driftwood off the beach in Devon. The design was along the lines of a Cape Anne dory with sturdy lines and a long keel. He tried to make his first keel out of ferrocement which exploded, so he then had to make another out of lead. While my theoretical knowledge had advanced in leaps in bounds from *The Odyssey* to the intricacies of high tech navigation which in those days was radio direction finding, I doubted my abilities to build a sailing boat and in any case, I was in more of a hurry to get down to the sunny Mediterranean. The problem was I had £800 to buy and equip a boat and my girlfriend Bridget, who knew more about sailing than I did, thought it a madcap idea.

I grew up for a while in Tokomaru Bay on the East Cape of New Zealand just north of Gisborne. Tokomaru Bay is a wild remote area still, a depressed area with little work and a population much reduced from some 1500 in the 1950's to around 400 these days. Most of the population are maoris from the Ngati Porou tribe with just a small pakeha (white) minority – when I was at school here I was the only pakeha in the class. It may have been in Tokomaru Bay that some seed to do with the sea and messing around in boats was planted. We used to make canoes from old corrugated sheets nailed together onto a bit of two by two fore and aft. Another bit of two by two was wedged amidships to hold the corrugated iron apart. The nail holes in the old corrugated iron were plugged with bitumen scooped up on hot days from the only paved road running around the bay. We campaigned these craft on the Waiapu River where it was held up on the beach and formed a bit of a lagoon. Only once did we try them in the surf with predictable results. The seed had to come from somewhere, I guess, as no-one in the family has anything to do with sailing at all, in fact nothing to do with boats of any description.

Or at least so I thought until 1983 when I was back in NZ and pestered my ill father to tell me how Grandpa Heikell had arrived in NZ.
Can't tell you ...it's a family scandal.
Given that most of the family was riven with scandal anyway, this seemed a bit rich, so I pestered him further.
Well if you don't tell anyone ... he deserted off a Finnish whaling ship down at Bluff.
I whooped for joy. Someone in the family had actually had something to do with sailing and real rufty-tufty square rigger stuff as well.

With my mother I moved to Auckland and had little to do with sailing except for one memorable time. My mother used to clean for a family of doctors in Mt Albert in Auckland and somehow the matriarch, Alma Morgan, persuaded one of her sons to take me sailing on the family boat. I think it was called *Kotuku* (an indigenous white heron) and it would have been somewhere between 25 to 30 ft long, an old kauri long keeler. The son had a friend along and it was pretty obvious I was an unwanted passenger. They went down below and left me steering in shifty following winds and not surprisingly I accidentally gybed a few times, though I had no idea what a 'gybe' meant in those days. Not surprising too that young Morgan was getting pretty annoyed with having to pop out and tell me what to do to keep the boat sailing. In the evening we reached Coromandel and after a quick dinner at anchor we turned around and headed back to Auckland. I was given the leaky forepeak to sleep in and it wasn't long before I emerged wet through and seasick to vomit over the cockpit coaming.

You might think that would be enough to put someone off sailing, but as I sat in the cockpit under the stars with the boat slicing to windward, I felt an elation and some strange and unusual love affair beginning. I steered the boat while the others dozed in the cockpit and began to understand the pressure of the tiller and the sweep of the water over the hull. There was chemistry there. Maybe I thought this was a one-off, but something itched under my skin and would come back later as a full blown rash – the disease of sailing small boats.

There was little other sailing. In the rest of the world there is a much received stereotype that all New Zealanders grow up sailing and while some do, the majority do not. Through school and university I did little sailing, a bit of crewing on Stuart 34's in Auckland, a bit of sailing on a Paper Tiger 18ft catamaran that belonged to a girlfriend's father, and a couple of times on a Mullety, those wonderful centreboard fishing boats that used to race back to harbour to be first in with the catch in the 19th and early 20th centuries. You couldn't say there was any overwhelming ambition to go to sea in my early days. But somehow in Buckinghamshire a worm was at work dragging me away from some orthodox career towards the sea. Call it sloth or call it by any other name, the history of personal ideas hardly ever corresponds to the story told afterwards. It just is.

In my old VW beetle I scoured the coast of England. With Abba and Tony Blackburn in the background I looked at all sorts of boats. The price of petrol had soared by some 70% to 72 pence a gallon and it seemed like I would swallow up my small amount of capital just driving around looking for a boat. Some of the boats like the magically named *Roc*, a small ferrocement boat named after the Persian mythological bird of prey, were just not going to work. The idea of 28 ft of bad ferrocement didn't seem viable and the name pre-supposed a watery demise for the boat. Others were 'work in progress'. I looked at lost dreams lying around boatyards and converted lifeboats rotting on mud-flats. Converting lifeboats to cruising boats was all the rage and there was even a book devoted to the project.

Looking for a boat on a budget can drain the imagination and I was getting desperate. I could see myself settling down to some mundane job to survive the coming economic meltdown with just a handful of dreams and 'if-onlys' to keep me going. As Charles Violet put it in *Solitary Voyage*:
I am sure my well-wishers hoped I would take a nice snug job and settle down, perhaps in a Government office. I might even have bought a bowler hat. Instead I wanted to start wandering again, wandering on the water for choice, because there is no better way of reaching distant places than by voyaging in a small boat.

It didn't help that Bridget was at best luke warm about the whole deal. Part of the £800 belonged to her and she was more interested in staying in Woburn Sands than setting off on what she judged to be my crackpot dream of sailing down to the Mediterranean. I not only had to find some sort of boat to do it in, but also had to convince her that it was viable to do so or end up owing £400 with no discernible way of repaying it.

2 Roulette

> FOR SALE   20ft sailing boat. JOG design.
> 2 berths. 4 HP Stuart Turner. 3 sails. £800 o.n.o.

I found *Roulette* in the classifieds of *Practical Boating*, a magazine long ago swallowed up in the fight for distribution figures. She was ashore in Southampton in Dyers Boatyard and young Jim Curry was selling her. Much later, in the late 1980's I think, Jim Curry was to achieve infamy in the national newspapers where he became Captain Curry and Captain Calamity rolled into one when he was rescued off his boat trying to sail to Ireland. That seemed a little unfair to me as Jim knew far more about fixing boats than I did. In later years when I met him again he was still modifying a small boat so that it was impregnable to seas should it get rolled or pooped. The last one I saw in Plymouth had a companionway modified to be something like a lifeboat with a perspex hatch that could be bolted down from inside. Jim reckoned he could survive a total knock-down.

In 1975 he was selling *Roulette* to buy a 22 ft Van de Stadt Pandora, a fibreglass beauty in my eyes, but out of my range. *Roulette* was built in 1954, well so I was told. The design was allegedly a Junior Offshore Group design, though nobody knew who the designer was. She looked very similar to the Phillipe Harlé designed Muscadet, built from plywood sheets on solid frames with a single hard chine. She wasn't pretty in the way that other classic little yachts were pretty. For a start she had a reverse sheer that was popular at the time to give more accommodation inside. She also had the coachroof built right out to the sides in common with some Maurice Griffiths designs. Inside there was sitting headroom only. What she had was a price tag of £600 after a bit of haggling and to my eyes that made her beautiful.

One of the things that had become readily apparent to me was that looking at boats soon produced the green monster of envy. While I looked at shabby and uncared for boats it seemed all around me were beauties ready and waiting to set off to sea. The problem was money and I didn't have enough to even put a deposit on one of these beautiful lovelies. It also became apparent to me as I prowled the marinas and boatyards that these boats hardly went anywhere except for a few weekends and maybe a week or two in the holidays. These were toys that were infrequently used whereas I was looking for something that I could travel on to the Mediterranean.

I'm not sure how I persuaded Bridget that this was the boat. Perhaps it was bluff and perhaps it was luck or perhaps she was tired of me talking endlessly about sailing to the Med. *Roulette* was hauled out in Dyers Boatyard near Cobden Bridge on the Itchen River. A ramshackle arrangement of moorings was home to various liveaboards and true to the liveaboard name, most of these boats were basically houseboats. They all treasured ideas of sailing off, mostly down to the Mediterranean, but in the event none of them did. When I turned up and reckoned I was going to sail down to the Med they all nodded sagely and reckoned there was another liveaboard in the boatyard, though in my case I had by far the smallest houseboat on the block.

I moved on board while *Roulette* was still hauled out. In the morning there was a quick run to the loo in the freezing cold before some sort of breakfast. To get some more money together and fund improvements to the boat I took a job in a local cough mixture factory in Southampton. Cough mixtures in those days had chloroform in the formula and the government had decreed that you needed two qualified people to check the quantities off when it was being mixed before bottling. With a science background and two years working as a lab technician in NZ I was vastly over-qualified, but managed to convince the employment officer of my intense interest in the field of cough mixtures and the cosmetics that the factory also made. The job gave me lots of time for reading at work so I taught myself the rudiments of navigation and the finer points of preparing a boat for small voyages.

Roulette had an ageing Stuart Turner 4 HP petrol engine with a centrifugal clutch. I later learnt the engine had first seen service pumping petrol on a fuel tanker during the War and had later been more or less marinised. It was to be an erratic runner. The two stroke engine was simplicity itself and I stripped it down and put it back together again in less than a day. It started, ran, stopped, wouldn't start and so began my long love-hate relationship with the engine. It was a temperamental beast that had several little two-stroke habits you had to know about. It had to be coaxed into life. Like all two-strokes it didn't like starting when it was hot however much you swung the crank handle. Even when luke warm it was easy to flood the engine, a symptom betrayed by the smell of petrol all through the cabin. Undo the float bowl, drain it, put it back on. The needle valve and seat needed to be as clean as a whistle, partially because the needle guide was worn. And the centrifugal clutch, in theory it disengaged at low revs, often didn't. The engine was fed from an old brass Seagull outboard tank mounted in the cockpit that held maybe quarter of a gallon of pre-mixed petrol. With another couple of tin cans of petrol *Roulette* had a total fuel capacity of 2½ gallons or so, about enough to motor 50 miles in a flat calm if I didn't waste too much cleaning out the float bowl.

Of electrics we had none. *Roulette* had no electrics at all, no battery and no way of charging it. Light was by a pressure Tilley lamp which also provided some heat and any other light was from a torch or a Camping Gaz lantern. The galley was amidships at the forward end of the boat and consisted of a gimballed Camping Gaz cylinder with a single burner on top. The wash basin was a plastic bowl that fitted into a round hole in a bench. To empty it you stood up in the forward hatch and poured it over the side. Water was from a two gallon plastic jerry can held by bungee cords in the galley.

When I think of what my present boat *Skylax* has in the way of electrics and other systems the comparison is frightening. *Skylax* has a battery bank of around 650 amp-hours. There is a dedicated engine start battery and a dedicated anchor winch battery. Power is needed not just for lighting including navigation lights, but for the instruments, radar, AIS, the autopilot, the chart plotter, SSB and VHF radios, to run computers and the Hi-Fi system, the pressure water system, the gas solenoid, the list is so long and complex that listing it here makes me dizzy from my amp consumption.

On *Roulette* the only things that ran off batteries were a MF/SW radio and some torches and they were all zinc-carbon disposable batteries. It's been said that not having navigation lights for sailing at night or some way of calling for help is irresponsible and I guess in a way it is. But then being responsible would have meant I wasn't going anywhere.

Somewhere in my reading in the magazines I had come across Cascover where nylon cloth was glued over the hull of a boat with Resorcinol glue. I think the process had come out of W.W.II aircraft manufacture using plywood and Resorcinol. At this time in late 1975 there was a mention here and there of epoxies and I eventually decided to use nylon cloth, nylon was preferable to fibreglass because it was flexible and could move without breaking, and epoxy paint. I sanded off the bottom of *Roulette* and over a week primed and painted on the cloth with epoxy paint, around five coats as I remember. Each coat had to go on after 12 hours but before 24 hours and all of it had to be stippled into the cloth. The process worked wonderfully, well it was a dirty and dusty long business, but with a good result. It was to prove invaluable later on. And if only I had known I was ahead of the game using epoxies in this way in 1975.

Bridget arrived down at the beginning of 1976 and the two of us lived on board *Roulette*. She got a job in a local chandlers which was useful as she got a discount on items in the shop and we were able to purchase our main item for dead reckoning (DR) navigation, a Sestrel grid bearing compass. The term dead reckoning has a bit of an ominous tone to it, presumably if you didn't reckon right then you were dead. I swung the compass in Southampton Water and worked out a deviation card for it.

Apart from the compass we had a few charts marked 'NOT FOR NAVIGATION' stamped in red across them. And a copy of Reeds Almanac. Ever optimistic, I had bought a copy of H.M. Denham's *The Tyrrhenian* and *Ionian to Rhodes* covering the west coast of Italy and the Ionian in Greece. Boat speed was estimated by looking at the water flowing past and after a few weekends on the Solent we got pretty good at working out boat speed. We could get it right to within half a knot or so and reckoned we could even do plus or minus quarter of a knot after a bit of practice. Using compass direction and speed through the water we could get a DR position and over time work out what our anticipated arrival time was at a destination. Picking up a light characteristic at night or the lay of the land by day and any conspicuous objects that could tell you where you are would hopefully locate a harbour or anchorage. Any useful navigation buoys or lighthouses also helped. A lead-line was used for depth by 'swinging the lead' as ships have done for centuries.

By June 1976 I reckoned we were ready to head for France. We had sailed *Roulette* around the Solent and anchored in all sorts of places. The engine worked mostly and I could usually get it going, with some cussing, to get us back up the Itchen River to Dyers Boatyard. To get to and from the boatyard the mast needed to come down so we could fit under some low bridges and to this effect it was fitted into a mast-step with a bolt through the foot of the mast. When Bridget let the forestay off I walked the mast down until it slotted into a cross brace that supported it and we lashed it down with some rope. The sails on *Roulette* were all cotton and fairly old, but they would have to do. At least we could sew them up fairly easily and so we did, though Bridget was better with a needle and thread than I was.

Most of the other jobs had been done like fitting a new bracket for the tiller, yes that bracket, and constructing a rudimentary chart table inside. Over the previous months we had been stockpiling food, rice, pasta, milk powder, tea and coffee, soya TVP meat substitute, cereals, biscuits, and tins of fruit and vegetables.

1976 was the great British summer with temperatures in the high 20's and low 30's and eternal sunshine. The countryside turned brown in the drought and the parks were full of sun-lovers in skimpy Speedos and floral bikinis. Bell-bottom trousers were out and mini-skirts and halter tops were on the decline. Van Morrison and Fleetwood Mac were on the radio and an embryonic Punk movement was around the corner. Life seemed so good and I had to wonder why we were leaving the long hot summer for a Mediterranean climate, though there were signs of trouble on the horizon. The pound had crumbled against other currencies and Prime Minister James Callaghan was struggling to shore up the economy in a country now described as the 'sick man of Europe', a term previously used for Turkey. Services were being cut and life looked like it was going to be bleak for a while. If I wandered what we were doing setting off in a small boat heading for some nebulous destination in the Mediterranean it might have been something more like escaping than heading towards somewhere. I really wasn't sure what I was doing.

When we announced we were going to cut the invisible cord that connected us to Dyers Boatyard and the other liveaboards there we got a mixed response. Mostly doom and gloom.

She's too small.
You'll be back – you wait and see.
What makes you think you can get to France in that.
Forget about the Med sunshine.

For whatever reason in my make-up, I usually shut up and listen and then silently vow to give it a go anyway. Stubborn would be a nice way of putting it. Tunnel vision might be more apt. I also figured that all the talk around the boatyard was just that, talk, and there were a lot of 'gunners' there. In NZ a 'gunner' is someone who is 'gunner do this, gunner do that', but years later is still propping up a bar in the same place.

For some reason and I'm not sure I knew what it was then, we decided to sail from Yarmouth to St Malo in one go. This is a distance of around 150 miles if you sail directly along the shortest route. From St Malo we intended to enter the French canal system that cuts down across Brittany to the Loire and so out into the Bay of Biscay. Then we would potter down the Bay of Biscay to the Gironde and cut down through the Canal Lateral à Garonne and Canal du Midi to the Mediterranean. Once there we would see how far we got.

3 The Channel

We set off from Yarmouth on August 25th with a favourable forecast and a lot of apprehension. Neither of us had ever sailed this far before. We had never sailed out of sight of land. And the weather had turned. The lazy sunny days of June and July in 1976 had clouded over with thunderstorms and torrential rain that soaked into the parched earth of England. We watched the weather and finally decided there was a window that would let us get safely across the 150 miles to St Malo.

Leaving harbour is always a wrench. I get a twisted gut from the apprehension of it all and turn into a semi-autistic soul concentrating on the boat, watching the horizon, the sails, the sea and listening to every noise the boat makes. I still do. On *Roulette* we were both quiet as we cleared Yarmouth and sailed off out of sight of land.

I always try to busy myself on board checking that things are working properly, the sails are set nicely, patiently easing the boat through the swells, a sort of displacement activity away from the enormity of the trip. On *Roulette* we did watches of three hours on and three hours off. It was always necessary to have someone helming as there was no self-steering and the boat didn't hold a course well if you let go of the helm. Still there was a lot of adrenaline around and that kept us going through the first night.

By day two the wheels had fallen off my trip. I was seasick, lethargic, useless, a passenger on a trip that was supposed to feature two explorers setting off into the blue yonder. I recovered and then we were faced with the sluice gate at the Roches Douvres. It felt like a miracle surviving the rocks and reefs and we were both gob-smacked. Literally unable to say anything until we both started laughing hysterically. And then we looked back at the rocky pinnacles and the lighthouse and were silenced again.

A little wind got up and we sailed in what I now hoped was the right direction to St Malo. My chart of the Channel now had a big dog-leg on it where the French frigate had given us our position and I had eventually worked out the problem with the steel tiller bracket and where the compass was sited. There was still no land or visible landmarks in sight.

That night there was the mother and father of all thunderstorms. We took down the sails and both of us huddled below as lightening hit the water around us. It wasn't supposed to be like this. On our one offshore passage it seemed like the gods were throwing everything at us. Where were those balmy Solent days pottering around the Isle of Wight and Southampton Water? We were both apprehensive and at every clap of thunder we both jumped a little and held on to the bunks. And yet we both felt somehow more optimistic about the outcome than we had when we left Yarmouth four days previously. The next morning was calm again and we sailed slowly towards St Malo. We could see land which was a bonus and around lunchtime a fishing boat chugged out of the light fog towards us.

Où est St Malo?
I gesticulated with an open palm sweeping halfway around the horizon.
The fisherman shrugged with Gallic nonchalance and pointed into the haze.

C'est combien des milles?

He shrugged and pointed again. Navigating by ear was evidently not working that well, but his vague direction pretty much agreed with where I thought we ought to be headed. We sailed on slowly and the great walled city materialized from a vague gray into solid granite. St Malo.

I got the engine started and we motored in to tie up on a pontoon in Anse Bas-Sablons. We were both knackered and were asleep below within minutes of tying up. Some six or so hours later I woke up and went outside to check on things, orientate myself, touch earth and bless whatever gods had brought us safely here. My heart skipped a beat and bewildered I looked up at the cast iron ladder seemingly miles above us. I'd forgotten the tides here are over 12 metres, 40 odd feet, at springs and for a moment I wondered if some imp had played a trick on us and we were tied up somewhere different to where we had arrived. I woke Bridget and we marvelled at the power of the moon shifting so much water, the same water that had picked us up and carried *Roulette* through the Roches Douvres. We made tea, oh so English, and retrieved the cake from the bilges that Bridget had baked for my birthday on the same day we came through Roches Douvres, and settled down to tea and cake. The cake was a bit salty, but still tasted like the most divine cake I had ever had.

Our idea from here was to potter through the Brittany canals to the Loire and the Bay of Biscay. From St Malo we pottered up into the Rance and sailed around this wonderful inland area hemmed in by the Rance Barrier and the hydroelectric plant that harnesses those huge tides. We had hitch-hiked through France a few years before after arriving in Europe at Genoa. Arriving by boat was something else, something special, a something that was beginning to find a home in my brain.

Living on board and travelling on the water, like some aquatic snail carting around your own home, going ashore for provisions and to stretch your legs, was becoming a way of life that somehow suited me.

It must seem bizarre after the calamitous trip across the Channel that we would settle into life on a small boat as if this was the most normal thing in the world. I don't have any explanation for this. The events, even after all these years, are seared on my brain. Not just the navigation cock-up with the compass, not just the encounter with the Roches Douvres that could have ended it all, could have ended our lives, but my own seasickness and my own folding in on myself. And yet this encounter with my own demons formed something in me. A resolve to conquer it all and continue with this life. Really it's a mystery and somehow life as a sailing gypsy seemed to suit me.

While pottering around in the Rance we had heard a disturbing rumour from other sailors in the area. The Brittany canals were closed and would not be opening until it had rained enough to fill the reservoirs. The long drought of 1976 had closed the canals for the first time in living memory and when we arrived at Dinan a short distance up from the end of the Rance the damage the drought had done was all to evident. Dead fish floated on the surface and the smell of rotting vegetation and dead and dying fish was enough to make you gag.

What to do? After a few days talking with the locals and the friendly harbourmaster it became apparent that we wouldn't be going through this side of October or November. So we decided to leave *Roulette* in Dinan and return in the Spring. We covered her up as best we could with some old plastic tarpaulins and asked the harbourmaster to keep an eye on her. We patted her topsides and hitch-hiked to Calais to catch the ferry to Dover and a bus to London.

Over the winter we lived in a tiny rented room in Golders Green. The cooker and sink were in a cupboard and the bathroom was down the hall. You needed to make sure the Israeli boarder wasn't taking a bath or you could wait for hours to get in. Bridget took a job in a tea blending warehouse on the Thames while I got a job working night shift in McVities biscuit factory in Harlesdon. Recession was biting in 1977, with inflation in double digits and union unrest rumbling on the horizon. Even the Queen's planned Silver Jubilee celebrations looked troubled when in February Idi Amin, the bloody dictator of Uganda, threatened to bring hundreds of dancers and supporters to 'help' celebrate the Silver Jubilee.

Night shift in McVities was by comparison quiet and sane. I packed boxes of biscuits and cakes onto a pallet. There would be long interruptions while the wrappers were changed for one supermarket or another. The biscuits were the same but the wrapper might be McVities, Sainsburys, Tescos or Co-op. Only Marks and Spencers had their own ingredients and white-coated overseers who would diligently wander around keeping an eye on quality control. Most of the night shift workers were Afro-Caribbeans from Jamaica, Antigua, and Barbados who called me 'Sharky' because I went sailing. Don't ask me for the connection.

Stacking the palette took no time at all and I taught myself to read in short bursts of a couple of minutes between the boxes piling up on the conveyor belt to the point where I needed to stack them up. It's harder to do than you might think, but in the end I could get through a book a night. After several weeks the foreman, a whitey we hardly ever saw, came over to tell me I couldn't read while I worked. I protested that I was still doing the job and didn't see why not. A couple of my bro's overheard him and he was soon surrounded by half a dozen of them threatening to walk out if 'Sharky' wasn't allowed to read his books. He backed down.

After the compass 'incident' crossing the channel I figured we needed to augment our navigation instruments so I bought a hand-bearing compass that could be held well clear of any metal bits that might cause it to deviate and it would also make getting a 'cocked hat' easier than using the grid on the main compass. You get a cocked hat by taking three bearings at different angles from known conspics ashore and draw a line along that bearing on the chart until they intersect. The size of the 'cocked hat' triangle gives you an idea on how accurate your position is and at worst you know you are somewhere in that triangle on the chart.

I also bought a few more charts and a portable short wave radio. The latter I bought after reading in one of my night shift books of a navigator who located the West Indies by tuning into local radio stations and getting the name of them and then turning the radio on its axis until he got a point where the signal was best and another where it was worst. Effectively he was using his MF radio as a radio direction finder. The null point where the ferrite rod antenna gives worst reception is the direction where the transmitter is. So you could get say 'Antigua Reggae Radio' and once you tuned into it, find where the signal was worst and head for it. In fact we hardly ever used it for this purpose but it did lead to a life-long addiction to the BBC World Service.

4 Through the Brittany Canals

We arrived back to *Roulette* in March 1977. Snow covered her tarpaulins and it was bitterly cold. *Roulette* had no heating so we dressed up in everything we had and wandered around like Michelin Man, occasionally ducking into a café for a coffee and warmth. Dinan was a very French place in 1977. The great invasion by Englishers snapping up houses for second homes had not started and there was not a real estate agent in sight on the High Street.

It took less than a week and then we were off through the Canal d'Ile et Rance towards the Loire. *Roulette* has only three foot draft so it seemed perfectly feasible we could get all the way through the waterways where the minimum depth is given as just over a metre. The weather had changed and we motored along in the Spring sunshine with the Stuart Turner popping away down below. The engine seemed to like the canals. We liked the canals. Life was sweet.

Between the late Winter/early Spring weather and the verdant countryside this all seemed something more akin to the summer idyll I had dreamed of. The banks were covered in flowers including the purple fritillary which is rare in England. Green woodpeckers lived in the trees and every now and then the introduced coypu, the huge South American rodent that looks something like a beaver, would emerge from the water or watch us with his head just above water from the edge of the canal. Villages along the way were welcoming and the lock-keepers all friendly souls who sold us wine and vegetables from their gardens. It was so good that I could have stayed on in this bucolic landscape and it probably started my life-long love affair with France. Lunch was a baguette with brie or salami, dinner was a one-pot wonder of pasta or rice with mushrooms, chicken, squash, tomatoes, whatever we had been able to purchase or had on board. One-pot meals were easier with just one burner and this is a skill I have honed over the years. Risottos, stews with all the veggies in them, stir-fries, hot salads, all can be achieved with a single pot. Even today with a majestic four burners on *Skylax*, not to mention oven and grill, a one-pot meal is a triumph over washing up and no less tasty for its apparent simplicity.

It was just all so civilized and to cap it all the sainted Stuart Turner just chugged on and on... for now. The Brittany Canal is narrow compared to some others in France and there was no commercial traffic squeezing by. In fact there was no traffic of any sort, not other yachts or canal boats or even a punt with fishermen in it.

At the back of my head I was ever conscious that this was not proper sea sailing. This was not the Channel or even the Rance estuary. You could only go one way with navigation defined by the banks of the canal. I worried over how I was going to get on when we put to sea again.

The Canal d'Ille et Rance, the canal we are on, runs down to Rennes, the capital of the region. The early March days are cold, but mostly clear and out of the breeze the sun warms the bones. The canals are all mist sitting on the water and along the banks on the higher reaches are châteaus guarding the valley we are running along.

Rennes is all bustle and hustle with cars and mopeds roaring around as everyone goes to work or comes home. There are shops and the smells of a city and we celebrate this little milestone, properly a kilometre-stone I guess, with breakfasts of croissant and café au lait and a set menu lunch sitting down at a table in a little restaurant overlooking the canal.

From Rennes we continue on the River Vilaine which is canalised so it's not as if you are zipping down a real river. The navigable channel is buoyed and pretty easy to follow as the river winds down to Redon. This stretch is all gorges and châteaus and villages with quays where we can park *Roulette* for the night. It is one of the most wonderful stretches of inland waterways I've ever been on. The weather is chilly and in places where the valley closes in we wake up to ice on the decks. Heading south to the promise of warmer weather has yet to materialise, but still we are buoyed up by progress more or less in a southerly direction as the river winds down to join the Loire.

When we finally arrive at the Loire it is snowing and blowing half a gale. Somehow we get across the river to some moorings off Nantes and tie up to sit it out. It is freezing cold and blowing a solid Force 6 up the river setting up a nasty little chop that rolls *Roulette* around all over the place. We leave putting the mast up until things calm down and we can feel the ends of our fingers. Bridget has been doing some sail repairs on the mainsail and despite the fact she is below and wearing mitts, has got what looks like frostbite on the ends of her fingers, painful little pussy sores that hurt like hell and worse, she can't feel the ends of her fingers on the right hand. We wrap her fingers up in bandages and pray for a bit of warmer weather. Down below we have a couple of hurricane lamps burning to provide a bit of heat and condensation streams down the ports and cabin sides. The sunny Mediterranean seems some way off.

What to do with Bridget's fingers when we couldn't even get ashore in this weather. What to do when I get to St Nazaire and the great rolling Atlantic.

07-04-77 Arrived at Paimboeuf. Snow. Wind F6. Tide ripping out.

We sit on a mooring at Paimboeuf for a couple of days before the weather lets us get off to St Nazaire. The old German destroyer pens from WWII are impressive, massive concrete affairs, 5 metres thick on the top, that resisted all the aerial bombardment the Allies could throw at it. Blondie Haslar, one of the pioneers of solo yacht racing led a commando raid on the pens using kayaks, though sadly only two of them made it back and the raid was not a success. Blondie Haslar took part in the first OSTAR in 1960 and championed the junk rig. *Jester* was a modified folk boat with a Chinese junk rig. All controls were led to a single hatch and the rig could be adjusted from here. We could have done with such a system as *Roulette* had no guard rails which meant a scramble up over the cabin top to the mast or the foredeck. Somehow it never seemed to be dangerous, though that probably had more to do with ignorance than any practical knowledge.

Looking out from St Nazaire we can see the Atlantic beyond the lock gates. This might sound a little mad, but I was looking forward to getting out there.

5 Biscay

We are not really going to cross Biscay. We are going to coast hop down the French coast to the Gironde estuary where we will pop back into the French inland waterways. It might not be the stuff of a proper ocean crossing, but it has a bit of menace in it after pottering through the Brittany Canals. Over the years I've learned, usually the hard way, that a little 20 mile hop across to somewhere can turn out to be as hard as days on passage across an ocean. It just needs an adverse wind against tide and more wind than you thought there would be and to cap it all wind on the nose as well, for a day-hop to turn into a real trial of will and strength pitting your boat against the elements.

The 20 miles to Ile Noirmoutier turned out to be a bit like that, a watery test of us and the boat. We locked out of the huge sea lock at St Nazaire and once outside realised there was a bit more wind than forecast and a lot more wind than we could feel inside. Now the gates of the sea lock had closed so it seemed we should go. I could hardly go back and ask them to lock the diminutive *Roulette* back through again.

I reef *Roulette's* mainsail right down. Reefing is old fashioned roller reefing by winding the boom around with a handle and wrapping the main around and around it. The trick is to loosen the topping lift to lower the end of the boom a bit and then put a few wraps in. Then loosen the boom a little more and do the same again. Like all good theory it's easier done in harbour than bouncing around on the sea and a main reefed with roller boom reefing just doesn't give the best shaped sail. Even with care you get a droopy boom with a few deep creases in the sail.

We set off in a F 4-5 which fortunately is off the land and gives us a tight reach down the coast without too much sea. Gradually the wind increased until by the time we are off Ile Noirmoutier it is F6 gusting 7. This is a whole lot of wind for *Roulette* and we have to make a handbrake right hand turn to get into the marina at Noirmoutier. I scrabble to get the main down and under the tiny working jib we shoot into the channel leading to the marina. I'm praying that the Stuart Turner is going to start and it does. We tie up at a pontoon berth with the help of the harbourmaster.
You came here in that wind.
We nod.
Your boat is so little. You can stay here for free.
We nod and are secretly pleased that we have survived our first test at sea.

We leave the next day heading for Ile de Yeu. The wind is from the north, a gentle F3-4 and we are keen to get on and head south.

Ile de Yeu comes up where expected and I bless French buoyage which is ever so reliable. The little harbour at Joinville on the top of the island is choked with boats, but one advantage with a little boat like *Roulette* is that you can squeeze in where others can't and we tie up alongside a local fishing boat. He isn't leaving until the morning and indicates we are fine where we are. We go for a wander ashore and come back to find *Roulette* tied alongside another fishing boat. The owner holds up his hands in that typically Gallic shrug and I figure that maybe our French is not as good as I thought. Still nothing is broken and we get ready for an early morning departure to St Gilles on the mainland coast opposite Ile de Yeu.

1 Roulette

From St Gilles we have a longish hop of 45 miles down to St Martin on the Ile de Re. You might think that's no distance at all, but at 3½ knots, a figure we have reckoned on for passages, that's close to 12 hours and though the days are getting longer, it will be touch and go to make it in daylight.

17-04-77 0830 Motored out of St Gilles. Spinnaker up.

The spinnaker on *Roulette* is quite a small sail given the three quarter rig. I'm pretty sure that the mast is off the Dragon class, it looks the right height and configuration with the three quarter rig and jumper struts to keep the top quarter of the mast rigid. Now a Dragon is a tad over 29 foot long so plonking this mast on the 20 foot *Roulette* gives us quite a lot of mainsail to handle. With the spinnaker up we sashay down to St Martin. Even so we don't get in until dusk and worse, the tide is on the ebb. As the depths get less and less on the ebb I make a run at an alongside berth, but misjudge it. I go around for a second go at parking and slowly come to a halt on the bottom as the tide takes the water away from the drying harbour.

We look somewhat foolish in the middle of St Martin slowly tipping onto our side, but figure that at least it's sheltered within the stone walls of the harbour with no real swell. Still I'm a little worried as to whether we will come upright without the cockpit filling with water. We haven't done this before.

We need a few provisions and some petrol so I decide to go ashore. It looks a bit gooey on the bottom, but I have my trusty Wellington boots and launch myself over the side. The mud comes up to my knees and fills the boots. Black smelly mud that squelches as I wade ashore like some clumsy Leviathan. The locals ashore are more bemused than amused as I take the boots off and empty the mud back into the harbour. Fortunately there is a tap nearby where I can wash the worst of it off. I get bread and vegetables and a can of petrol and squelch back to *Roulette* carrying my boots hoping that the local louts haven't turfed bottles into the harbour.

Around midnight the tide starts to come in and *Roulette* starts gently rocking, promising buoyancy before the water lapped over the cockpit coamings. A few hours later we are upright and we turn in happy the boat didn't fill up with water.

It's a 10 mile hop across to La Rochelle from St Martin and we are soon tied up in the Vieux Basin with restaurants and bars scattered around the waterfront. We have promised ourselves a little celebration here sampling the delectable crustacean. While we are on a strict budget it does the soul and the taste-buds good to splash out occasionally. So we are a little nonplussed when the crustacean turns up sans salad, vegetables, sans any garnish at all. I protest a little to the waiter who simply shrugs and attends to other customers. So we eat the lobster and then go back to the boat for a little stir fry thinking next time we will buy the lobster and somehow cook it on board. It did taste good though.

We plan to try the passage inside Ile d'Oleron which is shallow with shifting sandbanks. I wander around the harbour asking for advice and get directed to Pierre on a 30 foot steely.
Come on board. Where do you want to go?
I explain.
Tres dangereux. Pas de profondeur.
He pulls out a chart and explains that you need to have calm weather and follow the channel marked with withies at the top of the tide.

His boat is a shining example of a French steely that has been everywhere. Pierre crossed the Atlantic to the Caribbean, roamed around the Greater Antilles as far as Cuba, and then returned home. He is setting off for the Mediterranean soon and like us will take the inland waterways route from Bordeaux to Sete. The saloon table in the boat is a huge mahogany driftwood plank he found on the beach around here. The rest of the interior is cobbled together from ply and second hand bits and pieces. It all works and Pierre tells me I should build a steel boat, maybe here in La Rochelle he says.

We set off early in the morning knowing we will have to anchor somewhere off Ile d'Oleron, probably past the bridge, to wait for the high tide in the morning. We find a spot to anchor and with 3 metres under the boat I reckon it's deep enough. Not quite. As the tide ebbs we touch bottom and the boat starts to settle on it's side. I'm fairly calm about it after drying out in St Martin, though there are some niggling doubts about drying out in more open water. The boat thuds gently on the bottom and fortunately we are not right over. It doesn't make for a good nights sleep though.

In the morning it's difficult to see the withies in the early morning light and we use the lead line to sound our way through the sandbanks. It all reminds me of *The Riddle of the Sands* and the *Dulcibella* wriggling its way through the Frisian Sands in the Baltic. Somehow, heart in mouth, we snake our way out past the sandbanks until I can see the Atlantic swell breaking in the outer passage. This doesn't look good, but as we slowly motor up I can see a gap in the breaking waves and, hurrah, a couple of withies either side. I nose *Roulette* out and we eventually get through into deeper water. That all sounds very calm and professional whereas in truth there was a lot more heart-in-mouth worry going on.

As we sail down the coast the low-lying land offers little in the way of landmarks to take a fix on and I'm happy when we can finally see La Coubre lighthouse. Still progress is slow slogging against the tide and we seem to be going backwards at times. There is little wind and visibility is poor with a light mist. By dusk we are still some way off and I decide to try motoring for a bit. We plug on through the dark and what has now become fog.

At around midnight I see some lights and what I think are buildings and head towards them. Thank god, we are going to make Royan after all. As I look up at the sheer side of a building I suddenly realise that this is the side of a ship being escorted out of the Gironde by a couple of tugs. What I thought were the lights of the town were the deck lights on the ship. I push the tiller hard over and shout to Bridget to get the torch and shine it on the mainsail. We don't have nav lights and the torch is our only means of showing where we are at night. We glide by the behemoth that almost certainly wouldn't notice if we had been crunched under its sides.

23-04-77 0300 Arrived at Royan. Motorsailed to Royan against the mighty Gironde. Hurrah.

We arrive with literally just a few drops of petrol left in the tank and tie up alongside the outer wall in the harbour. In Royan I ask the local yachtsmen what they do when the tide is on the ebb and they are entering the Gironde. Well we anchor they all say. We wait for the tide. I make a sort of 'duhh' sound. Makes sense. They are a friendly lot and one of them donates a set of tide tables for the Gironde.
Make sure you go down to Bordeaux with the flood.
I nod and resolve to do so having experienced the tides in the Gironde getting in here.

This is the last place we will have any decent tidal range so at low tide we clean the bottom and apply new antifouling. The antifouling is all the soft red stuff. I guess hard antifoulings and antifouling with TBT, a tributyl tin compound, are around, but the soft red stuff is a lot cheaper and works pretty well. We also do a few last minute repairs and have a farewell drink with the friendly yachties of Royan.

27-04-77 1300 Off the last Biscay chart. Bordeaux in 5 hours! Average of over 5 knots with the tide.

We tie up alongside in Bordeaux just before Pont de St Pierre. This is the old cargo quay, but it all looks dilapidated and run down and no-one comes to bother us. We are talking about an era pre-dating the fashion for waterside properties and the old dock area has been left to rack and ruin. We need to take the mast down here to get under the Pont de St Pierre immediately downstream and for the Canal Lateral à Garonne. I also need to give a bit of TLC to the Stuart Turner that has been bravely beating away, though not always in tune, for the last few days.

We meet a load of odd characters in the run down port area. The university is not far away and quite a few students live in the cheap accommodation nearby. A group of them are much intrigued by *Roulette* and the voyage so far, though in a more Gallic romantic sense than a nitty gritty 'how-do-you-do-it' way. They are an interesting bunch, mostly studying philosophy or history or the social sciences and we get invited to a party where the lecturers and students mix and drink a lot of cheap wine. Getting dressed up is a bit difficult with the limited wardrobe we carry on board, though fortunately that doesn't seem all that important to this lot. I meet a young black guy, a lecturer in the philosophy department. Black, well read, and a good dancer to boot. He had everything and I felt somewhat relegated when he moved on to talk to Bridget and then spend a lot of time dancing with her. I'm a crap dancer. I sulk a bit and wander outside to mull over the existential problems of getting down the Garonne River to the lock into the canal. Bridget eventually finds me and I ask her where her new best friend is in a churlish sort of way.

Don't be silly. He's gay and probably wanted to dance with you.

I eat humble pie and reflect on the man; well read, a good dancer and gay. He's got it all.

From Bordeaux we have around 50 kilometres on the tidal stretch of the River Garonne before locking through into the canal. I'm looking forward to a bit more brown water cruising after the delights of the Brittany Canals, even if a lot of proper sailors poo-poo the idea of using these inland waterways as a shortcut to the Med.

6 Through the canals to the Mediterranean

Taking the canals, the Canal Lateral à Garonne (now shortened to the Canal de Garonne) and the Canal du Midi cuts off the whole outside sea route around the Iberian Peninsula and transports us straight into Mediterranean France. This brown water cruising may be looked down on by real blue water sailors, but I like the intimacy of chugging through the countryside while still on the water.

With the mast down and lashed onto the pulpit and the cabin top I fire up the Stuart Turner and we motor off on the flood to the first lock some 50 km away at Castets en Dorthe. The sides of the river close in and there are overfalls from the current. Just getting through the bridge at St Pierre is a bit like shooting a rapid with the flood tide piling up on the bridge supports and then whooshing down through the arches. Once committed there is not much you can do about it except head for the navigable arch and keep the boat straight.

When you have the current with you it doesn't take long to get down the river. The only problem here is that it is a river and though tidal, you only get the flood for around three hours against the river flowing down into the Gironde estuary. This stretch of the river is quite narrow and much like being on a canal except for the current. Inevitably the flood dies and we are left motoring into the current of the river. Fortunately it is not too bad and we plug on to the first lock and tie up outside.

There is one other boat here, a racy looking 27 footer which is on a dash down to the Med to be based there for the summer. The owner casts a snooty eye over *Roulette* which, to be fair, looks a bit like a gypsy boat with all sorts of stuff tied on deck.

Once through the lock we are back into the lazy hazy days of canal cruising. We could feel it getting warmer and the Med called with promises of rays and lotus eating. The warmer days are not doing the Stuart Turner too much good and it is back to its old impetuous behaviour of refusing to start when it's hot. Most of the locks in the canal are automatic locks with traffic lights to tell you when to go. As you approach the lock a handle suspended from wires across the canal hangs down far enough so you can grab it and give it a twist. The traffic light stays red, then goes green when the lock doors have opened. It was at about this stage that the Stuart Turner often decided to stop.

Two stroke engines like the Stuart Turner don't like to sit around on idle and eventually just stall. They don't like starting when they are hot. In *Roulette* I would hang around fairly close to the lock gates and then if the engine stopped we would each grab a dinghy oar and paddle her in. Any spectators on the banks or around the lock would watch amazed as we sat perched on either side of the coachroof paddling like billy-ho. Mostly it worked a treat. Once the lock cycle was complete and the gates had opened we could usually haul her out with one of us pulling a line on the lock-side.

This stretch of canal runs through the rich agricultural plain of the Aquitaine region. It's all vineyards and orchards, sunflowers and maize. There are village quays to tie up to or we sometimes nose into the bank and take a line ashore to a tree. Sometimes we can get the boat alongside, but mostly it's too shallow to do so. Given there are only a few working peniches left on the canal this isn't too much of a problem though when a peniche does pass it sucks a shed-load of water away from the bank and puts us on the bottom. Then the water comes back with a whoosh turning *Roulette* this way or that.

Along one of the stretches of the canal I detected a change in the note of the engine and on inspecting it discovered the water pump belt lying in a heap under the engine. I quickly stopped it and we coasted into the side of the canal. The belt was a strange affair made up of leather tabs and studs. You could add or remove a tab to make it longer or shorter to fit between the engine pulley and the pump pulley. For a while I tried to put it back together, but the leather had frayed so much it wasn't going to work. We would need a new belt though where to get one was a bit of a problem. In the end I used one leg of a pair of Bridget's tights sewn together to get us on a ways and pondered the problem of the belt.

I needed a few other spares including a float and the float needle valve for the carburettor to stop it flooding with petrol so, more in desperation than in hope, I penned a letter to Stuart Turner Motors giving them all the details of the engine and the spares I wanted. I added a Toulouse poste restante address – just in case. The nylon stocking, always mentioned in what I thought were apocryphal stories of a get you home fix when a fan belt went, worked a treat and only had to be replaced once with the other leg of the tights.

One of the amazing structures you come across on this canal is the aqueduct at Agen where the canal crosses a valley high above the river Agen. It's over half a kilometre long and has no real sides to it, just a footpath along one side. As you chug across the aqueduct you are looking straight down into the valley with the river running down the middle. This is all a bit scary on this old 19th century structure. After all it's just a masonry ditch sitting on arches high above the valley and you can't help feeling that canals aren't supposed to do this.

Toulouse marks the end of the Canal de Garonne and the beginning of the Canal du Midi, one of the oldest canals in France. We have given the Toulouse poste restante address to anyone who wants to keep in touch as well as to Stuart Turner for the spares. More in hope than promise I go to the main post office and find a package there from Stuart Turner. Inside there are the spares and the bill and a wonderful handwritten letter detailing the history of my engine. It was never a marine engine and had first been used to pump fuel from a petrol tanker in WW II. It had been marinised sometime after the war and put in *Roulette*.

I can think of few companies these days that would send parts off on spec to France without any pre-payment as well as keeping records and a history of all the engines they have manufactured. This is the sort of caring nerdiness and manufacturing pride I love that transcends the profit line that is so prevalent today. Sadly Stuart Turner went out of business some time ago, though you can still buy spares for the engines. Needless to say I posted a cheque back as well as a sincere letter of thanks. The nylon stocking came off and the engine had a proper water pump belt again.

Toulouse is all busy business and cars and mopeds scooting around the central basin. You don't have to go far to get anything, do the shopping, visit the daily central market, visit the bakers for crispy fresh baguettes or sit in a café for a morning coffee. It all goes on in close proximity to the basin where *Roulette* is moored and we celebrate what seems like the halfway point to the Med with that Toulouse speciality, cassoulet, in a nearby restaurant.

1 Roulette

Although it seems like halfway we still have to keep climbing up the locks in the Canal du Midi until we get to the reservoir at Port Lauragais. This canal is noticeably older than the Canal de Garonne. The locks are oval affairs which makes tying up alongside more difficult. The bridges are low arched affairs and peniches along this stretch have dis-mountable cabs at the back that can fold down so they fit under the low bridges. Along the sides of the canal are huge old plane trees that shade the canal and the tow-path. It is stunningly beautiful.

Many of the locks are manned and a lock keeper will often be responsible for two or three locks along a stretch of canal. When he has finished at one he jumps on his moped and like some mad trail-biker herves off down to the next.

On the descent from Port Lauragais we are in a lock around Trebes and waiting for the lock-keeper to open the sluice gates when he disappears shouting 'un rat, UN RAT!'

When he reappears he has a .22 rifle and starts blasting away into the corner of the lock opposite us. We both take cover as .22 bullets ricochet around the lock. He is still shouting in a demented sort of way while I am shouting back telling him to stop with a certain amount of hysteria in my voice. Eventually he puts the rifle down and opens the sluice gates and then the lock gates as if nothing has happened.

We get *Roulette* out of the lock as fast as we can and fortunately he isn't following on his moped for the next lock. We stop a bit further on and inspect the hull for bullet holes, but can't find any. I have to say in all my sailing days this is the closest I've come to being shot at. And in a lock on the Canal du Midi. Really strange.

The canal gently descends towards the Mediterranean from here with promises of turquoise water and light zephyrs wafting us along – or so I thought. These are lazy days, just the occasional peniche on the canal and less frequently a yacht heading to or from the Med. There are a few hire-boats around, but not many and for a lot of the time we have the canal and the locks to ourselves. In the locks we have devised a system where we take just one line ashore from the bows around a bollard at the top and back down to the stern where I can tighten or loosen it to keep us alongside.

The canal ends at the Etang de Thau though we have decided to turn off at Agde and exit into the Mediterranean along a short stretch of the River Herault. We duly turn off and find a pontoon to tie alongside while we get the mast up. This is all going to be something new. The Mediterranean. The big adventure. Turning *Roulette* into a sailing boat again.

7 Mediterranean France

11-05-77   *1445 Leave Agde.*
1530 Decide to go to Sete 12 NM further on.
Put spinnaker up.

The first day out in the Med is like the promise of a longed for dream. The sun is out, the wind is a balmy Force 3-4 and aft of the beam and the sea is gentle. Initially we were just going for a small sea trial, but once out there we decide to carry on to Sete.

I'm not sure I can put my finger on any one thing about the Mediterranean that has pulled me here. Yes I have read my Homer and the *Odyssey* figures in it all. That topsy turvy voyage around the Mediterranean sea taking on the gods and using guile and cunning to set his voyage home has a resonance that most people are familiar with. It speaks of a freedom that is removed from the grey working hours of the week and the grey waking hours of the weekend. There is energy and anarchy in the *Odyssey* that would be good to capture, to aim for, even in a small way.

There is something else that is often difficult to get across. In New Zealand you are miles from anywhere. Next stop going south is Antarctica. It takes as long to fly to Sydney as it does to fly from London to Athens. If you fly to Sydney it is not immediately recognizable as a different country. Everyone speaks the same language and the culture and conventions are similar. Not exactly the same, but similar. Australia is an amazing continent, a huge wild continent stretching from the tropics to the more temperate south. In Europe I still can't get over the fact that you can skip from one country to another, one language and culture to another, in such short distances. You can fly from England to Greece and step off into another culture that bears the hallmarks of the *Odyssey*. You can cross the Channel and breathe in French smells and culture. It is just so amazing that these countries all sit next to each other with the Italians jostling the French, the Spanish rubbing up against the Portuguese, the Germans next to Denmark. This geographical compression of peoples is a little miracle of diversity and choice.

Sailing to these places in this little capsule called *Roulette* has the feeling of an adventure. We live on board, albeit without being able to stand up inside, we use the wind to get around with occasional help from the engine, and we plot our own course to get from A to B. I can readily see that some people look at this way of life and express horror at why someone should subject themselves to it. It does seem a bit masochistic. And yet. And yet it is an adventure away from the received stepping stones to a career and some sort of conventional life. It has elements of the anarchy of the *Odyssey*.

We arrived in Sete and tied up alongside in the old basin. There are a few yachts here, some of them resident judging by the amount of seagull deposits over them, but mostly this is a fishing port. It smells of fish and the sea. The trawlers cream out day and night. Along the canal fish is for sale everywhere. One of the local yachties wanders around and asks us where we are going. We motion eastwards. He shakes his head and tells us that not only is a mistral on the way, but getting around the Bouches du Rhone, the mouth of the Rhone where it opens into the sea, is a long dangerous slog. It punctures our recently won enthusiasm for the Med and we decide to sit here for a bit and ponder strategy.

1 Roulette

I've read about the mistral and how it blows furiously out of the mouth of the Rhone. This is the wind that has moved locomotives down the track with its sheer force. It takes roofs off and blows trees over. It sinks small craft out in the Gulf of Lions. The next day dawns bright and blue and I wonder if the forecast can be correct. By midday it's blowing 40 knots out of that same electric blue sky. *Roulette* is pinned to the quay with the force and the fishing boats aren't going anywhere. I look out over the breakwater at the spray blowing off the top of the waves and check the lines and fenders on *Roulette* yet again. I have respect for the mistral already.

With a bit of research I've devised a plan to duck behind the mouth of the Rhone using the inland waterways and the mighty Rhone itself. This may be a bit of an attack of cowardice, but I'm not too worried about that. A new lock has just opened between the Canal Rhone a Sete and the Petit Rhone. As its name suggests, the canal runs from Sete through the Camargue to the Petit Rhone and then the Rhone itself. So we lower the mast again and lash it on deck and get ready to chug off into the land of the Camargue bulls, the very same bulls used in bull-fighting in the region.

We leave Sete in a blustery Force 4-5 that is soon gusting Force 7. We have a short motor across the salt lake of the Etang du Thau before we get to the entrance to the canal. The canal runs through the salt marsh and the low-lying reclaimed land of the Camargue so there are hardly any locks to negotiate. Once into the canal it's still blustery, but the water is flat and we chug along the short distance to Frontignan. We have to wait here for the bridge to open in the morning which is no sweat at all when we are tied safely alongside.

In the morning we are off motoring along the canal. It runs straight for long sections and with either etang or low-lying land we can see everything that is going on. Along the banks are little fishermen's huts that have grown into small holiday huts. The French evocatively call them 'Pieds dans l'Eau' and on the weekends they are out in force, fishing lines dangling in the water, coffee brewing and good cooking smells coming from inside, kids playing around the water and lots of cheery waves as we potter past. Once the 'Pieds dans l'Eau' thin out the etangs have lots of flamingos assiduously filtering water through their beaks for tiny shrimp and algae. Apparently the algae give them their distinctive pink colour.

This stretch of canal runs behind the huge purpose built marinas of La Grande Motte and Port Camargue that were built in the 1960's to foster tourism in the area. Behind the huge Port Camargue lies the original port for the area until the harbour silted and distanced it from the sea. Aigues Mortes is a huge fortified town and as you approach all you can see are the stone walls of the town and a few peniches and yachts moored underneath them. The town has been preserved virtually intact and until you enter through one of the fortified gates you can't see the town within. We dally a few days here, wander down the canal to Grau du Roi and the sea which perversely is now flat, and stock up on a few provisions before we push on into the Camargue.

The canal cuts through the marshy Camargue where herds of long-horn bulls graze, occasionally looking up to gauge our progress. The bulls are used for a quite humane form of bull-fighting in these southern regions. Rosettes are tied to the horns of the bulls and the participants try to retrieve the rosettes. On foot! And I've been told the bulls are fierce animals and shouldn't be approached in the wild. This form of bull-fighting is suggestive of bull-leaping in ancient Greece where athletes would attempt to vault over the horns of a bull and off its back. There is something of the Minotaur, of the spread of Greek culture and the folly of fit young men here.

There is little habitation on this stretch of canal with just a few farm buildings and the odd church spire indicating a village in the distance. The bucolic atmosphere is shattered when we come to the new lock that joins the canal to the Petit Rhone, an offshoot of Rhone major. This is a new commercial lock designed to take the super-sized barges that ply the Rhone proper and a bit of an oddity. The big barges are too big for the canal it joins onto. We tie up outside and trek along to the office to see the lock operator. He is both excited and nonplussed. We are one of the first yachts to go through, but we are also the smallest. When we enter the lock *Roulette* looks like a gnat perched in one corner of the huge concrete basin. Still the lock-keeper fills it up with a vast volume of water and we pop out into the Petit Rhone.

This is a wild stretch of water with trees and dense vegetation growing over the sides of the tributary. Herons and kingfishers sit on the branches and at one point the gaudy flash of a bee-eater darts across in front of the boat. We plug on against the current until we get to the Rhone proper and then arc around and into the mighty downstream current towards Arles. We moor up on a pontoon at Arles only just making way back upstream for the mooring against the current, the little Stuart Turner beating its heart out. There are a couple of other yachts here that have come down the central canals and we all chat about getting into the Med. It's about 40 kilometres from Arles to Port St Louis du Rhone where we lock out of the Rhone and into a short junction canal that leads to the sea.

Arles is a sleepy sort of place redolent of Van Gogh and his sunflowers and crows. I can remember a vivid illustration from a book by John Berger called *Ways of Seeing* that has a picture of Van Gogh's *Wheat Field with Crows* in it. You turn the page and the same picture is there with a caption saying this was one of the last works by Van Gogh before he committed suicide. Then you see the wild demons and manic crows as something else, a suicide note perhaps or a plea to understand the inner working of this demented genius. Not that Arles is all Van Gogh or Gauguin. The town is all old buildings and cafés shaded by plane trees where Van Gogh's Midi sun shines and the mistral rattles the windows when it blows.

It takes us no time at all to get down to the lock at Port St Louis du Rhone with around 3 knots of current under us. Once here we lock through and tie up in the basin at St Louis. We are back in the Med again. Well nearly. In Martigues just across the bay and up a short access canal we have some friends on a boat. I met Louise in New Zealand and on her return to Europe she met up with a French sailor, Olivier, who has a 30 foot wooden ketch that they live on in Martigues. For some reason, a foolish reason, I elect to motor across the bay to Martigues with the mast still lashed to the cabin. It turns out to be a bit bumpier than I anticipated in the bay and we scramble to put extra ties on the mast to hold it in place. It's a reminder we are not in the sheltered waterways even when it's just a quick dash across a couple of miles of sea. An elementary mistake to add to my stock.

In Martigues we are in a community not unlike that in Dyers Boatyard on the Itchen. There are numbers of boats here, all of them much bigger than *Roulette*, getting ready to set off around the Mediterranean or further afield. Most of them have been getting ready for years. We are accosted early on by Arthur, an Englishman with a nice GRP 30 footer.

Hullo. You aren't going to head off in this boat are you?
I mumble that we are. Arthur has a definite naval bearing and tone which turns out to be true.
Listen, I've navigated in the Mediterranean. It can get very rough you know. Your boat is not well enough equipped for the Mediterranean. You need to make some major modifications before you go.

I nod mutely and listen politely for another 10 minutes while Arthur, the professional, addresses me, the dilettante. Later I find out from Olivier that Arthur had his yacht transported by truck to Martigues and that his imparted knowledge is based on day-sailing out in the bay.

We stay on in Martigues for several weeks sharing suppers and long evenings on cheap red wine. We could have stayed longer, but despite Arthur's lectures about the boat and, I suspect, about our capabilities, it was time to move on. Mind you Arthur had touched a nerve after the Channel crossing. 'Harbours rot men and boats', they say, so we had another evening dissecting the sailing world over a few bottles of red and saying our goodbyes and steeled ourselves to set to sea again.

28-05-77 0830 Left Martigues. Motor down the canal and sails up in northerly.

All goes well sailing around to Marseilles and we are in the Vieux Port by 1800. Phew. There will be no more dodging into inland waterways because there aren't any. We moor bows-to on one of the pontoons alongside a massive motorboat. At least it seemed massive from a *Roulette* perspective. Mooring bows-to is the only way we can go as there is no reverse gear on the motor and I'm getting used to turning off the petrol as we come in and coasting into a berth with Bridget up front ready to jump off and stop the boat. It's a matter of not over-cooking it with too much speed and not stopping too soon so we can't get a line ashore.

Later in the evening we get a visit from the Gendarmerie Maritime.
You have papers for the boat?
I don't really, but offer the receipt for the sale.
Passports?
I get our passports out.
They look at our New Zealand passports and are a little confused. Then they hand them back.
You sailed here from where?
England. Southampton.
Now they look really confused.
In this boat.
I nod.

You need to be very careful here. It's better you don't go out sailing in these seas.
Now I'm looking confused.
We are going to the calanques next. And then along the coast. La Ciotat. Toulon. St Tropez.
One of them has been busy scribbling things down on his pad. They look at each other and finally turn away with the last word.
This is a little boat for these seas. It's better you don't go out from the port.

I Roulette

We are both a bit nonplussed by this. Bridget thinks they are trying to say we can't leave port. I think the same, but also figure that they haven't actually said we can't go or that they will keep us here under some law or other. If the forecast is OK we decide to leave in the morning.

By early morning we are on our way to Port Pin, a mini-fjord that cuts deep into the limestone cliffs. The wind is light and we ghost along still pondering the visit from the Gendarmerie Maritime and what they might do. These worries evaporate after a light sail and tying up under the steep cliffs of the calanque. We go for a first swim in the Med though the sea temperatures are pretty chilly so we don't stay in long. Bridget cooks up a chicken and noodle stir-fry and all seems well with the world.

We progress along the coast with benign winds to La Ciotat, and then onto Toulon. Only in the approaches to Toulon does the Med decide to test us with a bit more wind. It blows Force 5-6 from the north and we struggle to get into the basin at Toulon. It's a timely reminder that the Med is not all balmy breezes and hot sun. We struggle in behind the big commercial breakwater and somehow the Stuart Turner helps us motorsail up to the basin. A reminder it may be, but we feel OK reefing the girl down and bashing to windward. The harbourmaster helps us tie up in the midst of a motley collection of yachts ranging from racing machines to yachts being modified for passages with bits of off-cut ply and boat bits all over the decks. It all seems familiar and homely to be amongst this floating community.

Toulon is the main naval base for France and the waterfront reflects that. There are lots of shady looking bars and at night the ladies of the night are out and about. Actually they are out and about in the daytime as well. I'm not sure how it works, but in most of these harbours we have been waved away when we go to pay. Either we are too small or it's too early in the season or the harbourmasters are just very nice people. Still I'm not complaining on our budget. We do get a visit from the Gendarmerie Maritime again who this time don't suggest we stay in harbour and don't go to sea, but just record our details. I sort of get the feeling we are being watched. Then again I might just be a bit paranoid... or not.

While the authorities might be worried about us I feel we are learning our craft and becoming more competent at sailing *Roulette*. From Toulon we potter around the coast to Ile St Cros and then around into the Gulf of St Tropez. This is all fairy tale stuff because St Tropez is so redolent of Bridget Bardot, of the rich and famous who have lived here, of a lifestyle much read about, but rarely encountered. St Tropez is a little gem of a place that, apart from some big beautiful yachts in the harbour, seems somehow more ordinary than I expected it to be. I'm amazed we can tie up in the harbour and wander ashore to look at the place which has a bit more of the feel of a popular tourist resort than I imagined. Most of the cafés and restaurants are affordable and there are the sort of tatty souvenir shops you might find in less shi-shi resorts. But it's still St Tropez.

Coasting along on a boat allows you to make sense of the seascape and adjoining landscape. Driving around the coast your idea of the geography is blinkered by the confines of a road you must travel along. On the sea we plot our way and continually look at charts to position where we are. The two dimensional chart has to be turned into a three dimensional picture so you can locate a high cape, low wetlands, gently sloping hills and steep-to mountainous coastlines. There is a geographical wholeness to this and a church spire, a lighthouse, a wooded foreshore and the houses in a village all take on a significance located in space from our position on the boat. This is an intimate association with the physical world that I can't think you would get in any other way.

The coasting is all very well, but soon we will set off across to Corsica where all those conspicuous landmarks will be out of sight. We will be operating on dead reckoning again out of sight of land and I can't help feeling a little worried after our Channel crossing the year before. That was the last time we were out of sight of land.

8 Corsica

We left Port Cogolin in the Gulf of St Tropez with a benign forecast of Force 3-4 from the north. Since our course is around southeast this should give us a good slant to Calvi on the northwest corner of Corsica. It's something over a 100 miles so I'm hoping for just two nights out before we get there.

07-06-77 1000 Wind Force 6. Gusting higher.
Flying under just the storm jib.

The wind builds slowly through the morning and we progressively reef the sails until we have just the storm jib up. It's our only terylene sail and is tiny. And bright orange. By midday we are still zooming downwind to Corsica and the wind is still Force 6 and more despite the new forecast still predicting Force 3-4. By late afternoon the wind dies down to its forecast strength and I put the mainsail back up. We listen to the forecast again at 1800 and it has a regular sweeping interference that blots out the forecast every couple of seconds or so. The interference occurs on other frequencies as well which is a bit odd. Still we manage to hear enough of the forecast to know the winds will be light through the night and into the morrow.

07-06-77 1925 Wind dropping. Doing 3 knots in the right direction.

In the early morning light I spot a naval boat in the distance behind us. Through the day it more or less keeps station, sometimes cruising off in another direction, though a few hours later it is back slowly staying some distance off, but always there. When we are listening to the weather forecasts there is still the sweeping interference at regular intervals. The only thing I can think of is that some powerful signal from the naval vessel, most likely the radar, is sweeping us and causing the interference. If that's right these poor guys have been out all night trying to keep station at *Roulette's* sedate 2½ – 3 knots.

We carry on slowly through the day, the wind has died to just Force 2, with the naval boat popping up on the horizon every now and again. I would have thought we weren't much of a target with a wooden boat and wooden mast, so the octahedral aluminium radar reflector I have hoisted at the cross-trees must be working.

09-06-77   0010   Wind variable. Lightening on the horizon. Whale!!

That night the wind is variable and we make slow progress though still in the right direction. We have had dolphins around for most of the evening and I've got used to them. They come up and play quite close to the boat and then off they go before returning an hour or so later. Just before midnight I hear what I think is a dolphin getting nearer. And nearer. This is a big dolphin. And nearer. And then a huge black shape comes up out of the water around 20 foot off *Roulette* and blows a huge jet of spray. This is a bloody great whale and I'm close to having a heart attack. I try to call Bridget up, but my voice won't work and all that emerges are strange squeaky noises. Then a slightly hysterical 'Bridget' at least two octaves above normal comes out and she wakes, a bit grumpy at being woken up, and comes up into the cockpit. The thing is that the very big whale has now gone and we are sailing along sweetly in light winds.

It really was there.

Bridget looks at me a bit strangely and goes back down to sleep. I sit there steering on tenterhooks. The whale is somewhere out in front heading towards Corsica and I feel silly. Scared but silly because the whale was three times the length of *Roulette* and that glistening black mountain and its heavy breathing had looked like it could sink the boat without even noticing. I have read somewhere that old bull sperm whales come to these waters to spend their declining years here. Given a sperm whale can reach 50 foot and weigh 40 tons *Roulette* would look insignificant to it. The canny bulls bring along a couple of cows for company, so maybe the bull thought it had got lucky with *Roulette* and found a young cow.

09-06-77   0545   *Wind from the east and increasing. Time to put a tack in.*

Early in the morning the wind goes easterly and so we tack over. When we listen to the morning forecast on the radio the interference has gone so we assume our friends in the navy vessel have either given up or decided that we should make Corsica anyway. We sail through the day, though I am all ears when I'm up on watch in case my whale friend decides to visit. In the late evening we spot snow-capped hills in the setting sun. Land. We can smell it, smell the pungent herby aroma of the maquis even this far out at sea. As dusk falls we pick up a light and can identify its characteristic as the light off the entrance to Calvi. We sail on a bit and then heave-to so we can make landfall in the morning. I'm relieved we are more or less in the right place. Bridget is relieved as well.

In the morning we sail into the bay and by 1100 are tied up in harbour. From the little spiral bound notebook that was our log I see our top speed was around 4 knots and at times we were doing 1-2 knots. Speed was estimated by looking at the wake of the boat and we got pretty good at it so at times we would guess speed at ¼ knot increments. Our average speed for the passage was 2 knots, an average that seems like a snails pace for most people. We didn't really care. We had arrived in Corsica.

Calvi was a burst of Mediterranean colour and activity. There were other yachts around heading in all directions and ashore the bars and cafés buzzed. I get the feeling that something has happened, that we have gone through a door and I have been touched by the sun and sea and a change, a sea-change, has happened. We are like a couple of survivors sitting on a raft that has pitched up on an unknown island. We spend most of our time in the cockpit which is just about big enough for the two of us. At night we leave the hatches open and can see the stars as we go to sleep. I guess some people would think our life was primitive. I trudge off with the little jerry-cans for water. We wander into town for supplies and treat ourselves to a coffee on the waterfront on the way back. Our budget is limited so items like expensive cuts of meat and imported items are not on the menu and nor are the menus in restaurants. Eating out is a special occasion that we hum-and-hah about for ages. When it happens it is special.

Voyages can be like this. We have left behind the Cote d'Azur and Riviera, coasts that have long seen tourism. Busy Marseilles and naughty St Tropez are far away across the sea. Corsica is a wilder place, a place little touched by tourism, that has a hint of somewhere where you need to look after yourself. It may be just my imagination, but this island is much removed from the polite tourist coasts of Mediterranean France.

The town of Calvi perched on the bluff rocky headland has a fort at the top, an old Genoese affair, which is a base for the Foreign Legion. We had been a bit worried by tales of banditry in Corsica and of the Corsican Liberation Front that liked to kidnap the odd tourist or two. On mainland France we had been warned on several occasions to watch our backs. This was all a bit confusing and like a lot of places that get reported in the news as being dangerous, what always astounds me is the appearance of normality. The shops and cafés and restaurants are all busy-busy, the harbour has yachts coming and going, the buses run and the taxis tout for business. If there is danger here it is not apparent, though I guess danger rarely is.

From Calvi we headed up around the top of Corsica to the northeast side where I figured we could hop across through the Tuscan Islands to the mainland coast of Italy. The passage up to Ile Rousse was uneventful, The passage to St Florent less so. The weather was a gentle Force 3 for the sail up to the entrance to the Gulf of St Florent and all went well. As we approached the entrance the wind suddenly increased from the southeast and steadily rose to Force 7. Yachts scuttled back to St Florent under power with several of them coming in close to us and apologising for not being able to give us a hand. *Roulette* tacked on bravely into the early evening, but it was soon apparent we were making little or no headway and that the wind looked like it would keep blowing through the night.

12-06-77 2200 Anchored behind Cavallata. Lost several battens from mainsail.

I scanned the chart and figured we could tuck into a bay under Punta Cavallata. On the next tack I started the engine and we managed to round the cape and get into the bay. Somehow when dropping the anchor the rope rode caught around the propeller, though fortunately the anchor still held us. I dived over the side and disentangled it before getting back on board and watching us to see we weren't dragging. We weren't so it was time for a late supper and bed for one of us. We kept an anchor watch through the night.

In the morning the first light reveals wonderful turquoise water all around us. The wind has died to virtually nothing. I'm a little worried the propeller shaft may have been damaged when the anchor line got caught around it. On firing up the Stuart Turner everything seems OK so we chug off down the gulf to St Florent. It's a different place from the bumpy seas and wind blown spume of the previous evening. We feel pukka and happy about our situation. Funny how the human brain has such a small capacity for remembering bad stuff, even as recently as the previous day. When we arrive in St Florent several yachties help us tie up and fête us for arriving safely.
We have been worried about you in that weather.
We wondered what had happened to you because you didn't arrive here.
We feign a casual 'no probs' attitude and savour the glow inside that we made it safely. Small triumphs can be so good.

We relax in St Florent for a bit before we tackle the passage around Cap Corse. The cape has a bit of a reputation for confused seas and in bad weather is definitely a place to be avoided. The local yachties who welcomed us in ply us with horror stories about the cape. We say we will be careful and later meet the sanguine Jean-Pierre who has sailed around it often and who tells us that as long as we are careful with the weather there is no real problem. Yachty rumour is an odd thing where snippets and opinions are circulated and soon become fact. We are learning to sift through rumour and reality. The information is all proffered in good faith, it's just that much of it is hearsay and rumour that has somehow ossified into certain truth. We elect to listen to Jean-Pierre.

We left St Florent at 0700 in a flat calm. The forecast was for light winds and so it proved to be. We ambled up the coast and down inside Giraglia Island to arrive in Macinaggio Marina at 2000. From here we would island hop across to mainland Italy and then cruise down the coast of Italy to the Ionian Sea. Somehow it feels like we are really in the Mediterranean in the sense that it feels normal to be here. We feel comfortable in this inland sea and with its peoples. And we feel comfortable with this voyaging thing, like neophyte members of Odysseus' crew with the ghostly old navigator watching over us.

9 Italy

18-06-77 0845 Left Macinaggio. No Gendarmes following us this time!

The Italian island of Capraia lies just over 15 miles east of Macinaggio Marina on Corsica. You might think you could see it from Corsica and on a clear day you probably can, but a dusty haze in the summer means that you usually can't until a lot closer to it. We steer a compass course for the southern tip of the island in a Force 3-4 from the north, an ideal wind for *Roulette*. All around us we have fellow travellers, By-the-Wind-Sailors or Velella velella.

These jellyfish, more properly hydrozoans, are a community of specialised polyps that live in a symbiotic relationship. The dangling tentacles catch food, mostly plankton, that go to the digestive polyps, there are reproductive polyps and I'd assume polyps which form the distinctive sail of the community. They are readily recognized by their blue sails and the really clever part is that these little guys beam reach with the sail. So while all the other jellyfish are drifting with currents or pulsing water out to go in a particular direction, the Velellas are dreamily reaching across the sea. There are hundreds of them and we sail through a sea of the little polyp craft heading for Capraia or points further east.

Capraia is a prison island though you are allowed to moor at Capraia village itself. We anchor off with several other boats and roll in the swell creeping around the headland. The wind is blowing from the south, but the swell curving into the bay is on the beam. Somewhere I have read that if you rig a bucket on the end of the boom so it is full of water and then let the boom right out and tie it in place, this will dampen the rolling. Hmm. It probably works a bit, but overall it appears that this is a bit of a theoretical solution that doesn't really work in practice.

It wasn't the most comfortable rolling at anchor, but every now and again you just have to put up with it. Bridget cooked a great risotto and we went to bed early. I had modified the boat so that we could put an infill between the two bunks, an arrangement that sort of worked to make a half-double berth. The main problem was that neither of us was short of stature so our legs still had to go into the space where the bunks partially ran under the cockpit as demi-quarterberths. Even in hot weather there was nowhere to sleep on deck or on the cabin top and besides, the lack of guard rails made it a tad adventurous to do so.

19-06-77 0745 Left Capraia. Wind on the nose. Heading for Marciana Marina.

We left early in the morning and headed for the northwest corner of Elba, the main island of the Tuscan archipelago. It's a 22 mile trip, but with the wind on the nose the distance is going to be a lot longer by the time we tack to Marciana Marina. We are only making 2-3 knots to windward and if you do the maths on the actual distance sailed, at least 1½ times the straight line distance, then it turns into rather a long day.

Sailing ships in Greek and Roman times must have struggled to do what we are doing in *Roulette*. A square rig, the rig most often depicted on ancient trading vessels, would probably make little more than 90 degrees to the wind making it virtually impossible to get to where we are going unless the wind direction changed radically. You have to wonder what these old trading boats did. I call them boats because a typical trading boat from this era was around 40-45 foot. They didn't look like the boats often depicted in Homeric and later times with a bank of rowers on either side, rather they were tubby double enders not unlike a Colin Archer design with smaller crews, probably only enough crew to muster six a side and that would be just enough rowers to get them in and out of harbour or to avoid dangers for a short time. Certainly not enough for sustained rowing to the next destination.

I guess these trading ships would have sailed around hoping for a wind shift. Most of the boats would have a definite destination in mind and presumably specific items of cargo to trade or that they thought they could trade. Perhaps they just stayed in an anchorage until a favourable wind sprang up. One thing you can be sure of is that there were a lot of shipwrecks as these unhandy craft attempted to weather a lee shore or get into a harbour or anchorage. On *Roulette* we get something of a feel for this as our speeds are relatively low and there is always the distinct possibility that the engine is not going to start. Touch wood we have not wrecked the girl yet.

In lots of ways you get a better feel for what it was like trading in unhandy ancient boats in a little boat like *Roulette* than you do sitting in an Ivory Tower contemplating the sort of pottery found at a site on one of these islands and extrapolating from that. Trading items including pottery would often have arrived by different routes and possibly at much later times. An empty ship would no doubt stock up with whatever was on offer for an 'empty leg' including discarded junk that might just fetch a price elsewhere. These ships would often be more like tramping coasters than straight line freight carriers. In *Roulette* we rely on the same wind and sea and mostly on the same navigation techniques to get around navigating from island to island like stepping stones across the Mediterranean.

We don't get into Marciana Marina until 2030 and once tied up get some dinner on the go. Cooking on a single burner is an art. If you have several things to heat up on the gas ring then you need to plan what goes on first, what can be popped back on the ring afterwards, what pot or pan can be juggled with the other, heating one a bit and then the other. It might sound a bit boring, but in fact we ate well and were adept at improvising.

In Marciana Marina the buildings around the harbour are grand affairs, all Baroque and Rococo and hinting of affluence. In fact the whole island seems to have been popular with Italians who had enough money to build some spectacular villas and mini-palaces. We chug around to Porto Ferraio from Marciana Marina and tie up in the old harbour surrounded by the faded elegance of a town that has seen better days.

One of the advantages of small craft like *Roulette* is that the marineros running a quay tend to leave us alone. They wander around taking money from all the bigger boats and when they get to us hesitate, look at the diminutive yacht, shake their heads, and then wander on to the next yacht. There are some powerful arguments for cruising in small craft here. With a relatively shallow draught and a modest beam, around six foot, we can squeeze into places other yachts cannot get to. In marinas and harbours the marineros often don't have the heart to charge us anything, a statement that may sit strangely on the ears of other yacht owners, but true nonetheless. Add to that the lesser costs for maintenance and any new gear like a sail or cordage and you get sums that impoverished yachties like me can afford.

1 Roulette

The idyllic days of coasting in gentle zephyrs came to an abrupt end sailing down to Porto Azzuro on the bottom of Elba. In fact the whole adventure nearly came to an end. You often get little black clouds wafting around, squall clouds that drift across the blue sky, though we were never sure what they signified. In my experience so far they signified nothing, but then we were unschooled in the wiles and whims of Mediterranean weather. Sailing down the coast in a light breeze we put the spinnaker up and kept it up while a few of these little black clouds passed by with nothing happening. Until one of them unleashed a huge squall of wind and in a moment *Roulette* was on her side with the mast horizontal to the water. Bridget screamed that water was pouring into the cockpit. I clung onto the mast trying to release the spinnaker halyard, all the time with the boat on its side. I struggled to get the halyard off the cleat, eventually did, and pulled the spinnaker in out of the water. *Roulette* came upright and we got the mainsail down and then started bailing frantically.

The cockpit is not self-draining and there was a lot of water in the boat. I bucketed water out from down below and handed the buckets out to Bridget in the cockpit to empty over the side. They say there is no more efficient pump on a boat than a man in a panic with a bucket. It took nearly an hour to get all the water out of the boat and back where it belonged. Down below bedding, clothes, books and papers were a mess. By the time we had finished the squall had passed and *Roulette* was bobbing around in the leftover chop in no wind at all. Still we sat there, then had a cup of tea, and watched the sky for black clouds for a bit before putting up a reefed mainsail and keeping the spinnaker securely stowed in its bag.

We finally arrived in Porto Azzuro, slowly in a much undercanvassed *Roulette*, and tied up on the dock. Porto Azzuro used to be called Longone and had long been associated with the prison here. Its new name was designed to attract tourists and I wonder what government department gets the job of renaming a place and how they go about it. Do they call in all the old maps and charts and issue new ones with the name Porto Azzuro on it? Or does it happen gradually over time?

Our information came from my treasured copy of *The Tyrrhenian* by H M Denham. This was an early yachtsman's guide to the harbours and anchorages around this part of Italy. We read it carefully every day and worked out as best we could where our next stop would be. Denham had been in the Royal Navy including service in the Mediterranean and when he retired sailed around its shores in his yacht recording information for his books. His guide was invaluable and peppered with wonderful, almost Edwardian, comments along the lines of '… beware of the urchins here' and '… excellent wildfowl shooting reported in the marshes'.

Ancient sailors would have had their guides. Only a few survive, one of which is the Periplus of Skylax, dating from the 5th century BC. It lists harbours and towns around the Mediterranean with brief comments on who lived there and what the town or city was like. Importantly it also listed sailing times between places.

And after the aforesaid cape Malea, Side city with a harbour, Epidauros city with a harbour, Prasia city with a harbour, Methana [i.e. Anthana] city with a harbour. And there are also many other cities of Lakedaimonians. And in the interior is Sparta and many others. And the coastal voyage of the Lakedaimonians' territory is of three days.
Translation Graham Shipley

I Roulette

In fact I'd bet the boat that these ancient navigators also had maps of some sort. Drawing a map involves a knowledge of perspective, of spatial arrangement, the ability to translate a three dimensional view to a two dimensional view, and some basic geometry and mathematics. Drawing a map in the dust on the ground, on a dried skin or a piece of wood, on stone, on paper if you had it, is the most human of activities. It's the old 'a picture is worth a thousand words'. Less developed societies from the Australian aborigine to the Eskimo all have a detailed sense of the geography around them.

So in lots of ways our navigation is a re-invention of ancient techniques. There is no certainty of arrival at the next destination, more a hope that if we get things half right we will arrive in good time at a safe haven. We have a lesser interest in ancient shrines, though we visit some of them anyway, more out of curiosity and maybe just to be on the safe side. This coast is such a repository of ancient bric-a-brac that you can get overwhelmed by it all.

25-06-77 1800 Arrived Fiumocino. Choppy seas.

Arriving in Rome, well actually arriving in Fiumocino, the canal port for Rome, is a milestone. It had seemed so far away and now we were here, just a short train ride from the capital. Rome is like Italy times two. It is frenetic, loud, quiet, full of ancient remains and full of modern add-ons. The locals seem to explode with energy getting about and then slump into a café chair and spend hours contemplating an espresso. We became demi-Italians and went over-budget eating wonderful Spaghetti Marinara and contemplating our espressos. Between the food and the vibrancy of the Romans we were smitten with this life.

It had to end. Apart from the fact we couldn't afford to live the life, we wanted to get on down the coast. Our passage times were improving and we sailed down to Anzio in good time.

26-06-77   1600   Arrived Anzio. 28 miles in 8 hours!

On one other occasion we averaged 4 knots for a passage. Still most passages were around 2½ knots and sometimes less. Between the two of us we had melded into the boat. There was little shouting about what to do and we instinctively knew what was needed. We would let the main-sheet sheet off for a reef or if the boat had a bit much way on when going bows-to I would put a bit more pressure on the kedge rode. Mind you I guess there is not too much call for shouting on a 20 footer when you are not far away from the other person anyway.

Anzio has modern associations, relatively modern that is, for me. My father was here in World War II and fought in the infamous series of battles to take Monte Casino in the advance on Rome. The Allied troops landed here in Anzio and then proceeded inland towards the German defensive line. It was a bloody and costly affair and something of a débâcle for the intelligence gathering efforts of the Allies. My father was in intelligence and when I asked him about the campaign here I got a terse reply to the effect that '… nobody bloody knew where the Germans were'.

I didn't grow up with my father. He left when I was 9 and I saw him only sporadically. He did tell me I was lucky I was born at all. After Anzio the New Zealand troops were billeted on Ischia in the Bay of Naples and here he fell in love with an Italian girl, It was, he told me, a near run thing as to whether he returned to New Zealand to his fiancée or stayed on Ischia and married his

Italian sweetheart. It seems this life thing can be pretty hit or miss. Or maybe I would be writing this in Italian. Always hard to tell what that jumble of genes will do.

We arrived at Circeo just down the coast from Anzio and moor up under the high promontory of the cape. It literally goes straight up from the sea. This place is identified as Circe's Island in the *Odyssey*, the place where the enchantress Circe and her attendants lured Odysseus' men into her house and then turned them into swine. Odysseus, with the help of the god Hermes, defeats the enchantress and then he and his men dally with Circe and her beautiful attendants for a year. There is a powerful magic in these old place names. Capo Circeo is now connected by flat marshland to the coast, but it is easy to see how in earlier times it was an island just off the coast and how the channel separating it silted over time to connect it to the mainland. It's a bit like being a part of the *Odyssey*, sailing around a coast peppered with ancient place names from Homer's seascape.

For someone like me from New Zealand, which has little more than 150 years of European history, this coast of old forts and venerated temples and ancient place names is difficult to comprehend. History is heaped upon historical site after historical site adding up to thousands of years and this does my head in. That is in the sense that there is a lot to take in and to place the civilizations down the ages along with all the present day sights and sounds. There is a definite overload of information, though bit by bit I'm sorting all this history out and getting my history neurones in some sort of order. Well at least until the next fortified headland rearing up like some palimpsest of ancient bric-a-brac.

In Gaeta we come across fortifications en masse. The whole headland sheltering the bay is encompassed by massive fortifications, though they mostly date from the 15th century so are 'not really that old'.

29-06-77   0830   Left Gaeta. Turned back in strong headwinds.

Turning back when you have set out with all the expectations of arriving somewhere else is a difficult thing to do. It's like giving up. Or giving in. Like failure. And yet it is the sensible thing, the sane thing to do if you judge the conditions to be bad for boat and crew. Though when you turn around and skate back into harbour the relief is palpable. Sailing has enough masochism of sorts attached to it anyway, something non-sailors always ask about. Why do you do it? Why inflict this life on yourself? Sometimes it's difficult to explain and sometimes you need to turn around and try again another day.

Mind you the congruence of random events can make you wonder whether you should have persisted in the first place. We sailed down to Ischia in the Bay of Naples the next day in fine weather, congratulating ourselves on delaying by a day. Porto d'Ischia is an old volcanic crater that filled with water and had a narrow channel cut into it so it could serve as a nicely protected harbour. Approaching the narrow entrance to Porto d'Ischia I couldn't get the Stuart Turner started so we elected to sail in. The wind seemed fair for it and we gently angled into the entrance, all of 35 metres across, where the wind died. We ghosted slowly in, too slowly, as one of the hydrofoil ferries left from the basin to go to Naples. I angled *Roulette* towards the side to get out of the way and narrowly missed being run down amid lots of shouting and hooting, only to be dumped onto the rocks bordering the entrance by the wash from the ferry.

30-06-77 1800 Ischia. No engine. Nearly holed!

The crunch when *Roulette* hit the rocks was a sickening grinding sound and I was convinced we had been holed. We got inside and tied up and I immediately put a mask on and dived into the filthy water to check on the damage. To my surprise there was just a chunk taken out of the chine and some scratches and gouges in the ply. The epoxy and nylon cloth I had sheathed the hull in long ago in Southampton provided enough strength to hold it all together and limited the damage to minor superficial work. Inside and out there was no structural damage despite the poor old girl being slammed down onto the rocks.

In the Bay of Naples everything is dominated by the brooding shadow of Mt Vesuvius looming over Naples and the islands in the Bay of Naples. It's an active volcano and you can see it puffing a bit of smoke out every now and again. Living under a volcano seems to engender an atmosphere of 'what the hell' in the Neapolitans and their island cousins. They seem to be more anarchic, to live life for the 'now' and 'to hell with the future', even the near future. You can see this when you cross the bay which is littered with garbage, plastic bags, old wooden fish boxes, all sorts of awful looking rubbish as if they don't care about their environment. If the volcano is going to blow sometime, and it will, then why bother about it all.

We take the hydrofoil into Naples, quite possibly the same one that nearly ran us down, and wander around the streets of Naples. It is an edgy city and when we stop in one bar for a coffee somewhere in Naples, a lady sidles over.
You are English.
We nod. It's easier for us to say we are English than describe where New Zealand is.
You shouldn't be here. This is a bad bar with bad people. Come with me. I will take you down to the end of the street.
I can't say we felt threatened, but we heeded her warning and walked with her down to the end of the street.
Stay in the big streets.
So we did stay in the big streets where there was more than enough to see in this edgy bustling city without bumping into the bad people.

I'm happy *Roulette* is in good order after her bump and check her over for any other problems. There are always bits and pieces to fix, tightening screws and bolts and nuts up, a touch of varnish here, yet more repairs to the old cotton sails. It's never-ending this fixing bits on boats and yet it is rewarding in the way that we contribute to a safe onward passage. We are banking maintenance points, putting sweeties in a jar against future events where we will have to take them out and use them, trying our best to make sure everything works when the wind gods, who live nearby here, whip up the sea and make things hard on the boat and difficult for us.

We cross the Bay of Naples to Capri on the other side with gentle zephyrs and a sense of unreality as we sail through the backyard of the Romans, of Pliny and Tiberius and all the others. In Capri we tie up amongst a gaggle of big shiny motorboats. These gleaming machines probably use more fuel in five minutes than we have used to get down here from England. The marinero on the quay wanders along to collect his fee, a not inconsiderable fee I learnt later, and then thinks better of it and leaves the funny little English boat alone.

We spend a bit of time on Capri exploring the island and getting ready for the descent into the far south of Italy. The island has a hedonistic past mostly owed to the Emperor Tiberius who in his declining years lived here amid a coterie of young women and men who indulged in orgies inside the royal palace and in the gardens as well. It has an air of debauchery about it, but the visitors and the tatty tourist shops shift the mood away from the voluptuous orgies of Tiberius to something more cheaply pornographic where all you get is a priapic postcard of a young boy. I'm not being prudish, but silly postcards and chattering tourists don't contribute too much to wonder at the extravagant orgies Tiberius and his crew engaged in.

We leave Capri heading south. The little harbour of Acciaroli was 42 miles away and a long haul for us. It was a slow old trip though worth it. Acciaroli is a gem, stone houses clustered around the harbour with just a few local fishing boats in it.

05-07-77   2400   Speed 1 knot. Bang bang in light airs.

We left in the morning and sailed to Cape Palinuro and ghosted around the corner to Camerota. We had little in the way of detailed charts for the coast and with the wind dying I decided to cut behind the small island off Camerota. It had a single figure on my chart showing just over a fathom, about 2 metres, so I thought we would be OK. A little way into the channel the water shallowed dramatically and I cut the engine just before we ground to a halt. I jumped off into the shallow water and managed to turn *Roulette* around so we were pointing back out the way we had come. I fired up the engine and we gave the island a wide berth and arrived at Camerota in the early afternoon. It had been a tiring slow trip so we both crashed out down below.

An hour later there was a lot of thumping on the deck that woke me abruptly. I came up to find the irate skipper of a sword-fishing boat that had squeezed in alongside shouting at me. We were in his place and he was clearly upset. I spluttered that I hadn't known, we had just got in, we were tired, and where should we go. He pointed to a berth a few boats down and started to untie our mooring lines. Whew. I explained it would take a minute or two to get things ready. Too late. The skipper and his crew were already rudely shunting us along to the new berth.

I was a bit grumpy from being so rudely awoken and must have showed it. The skipper asked if we were all right there, then assured us we would be fine where we were, then with less severity asked if we would like some fish. What can you say. Yes please.

Alfio wandered up later that afternoon with a nicely gutted and filleted fish of some sort and also to warn us that a sirocco was forecast and would probably blow for 2-3 days. The sirocco blows at anything up to Force 7-8 from the south and so we doubled our lines and settled into life in Camerota. We had fresh fish for supper and we were the only yacht in a harbour otherwise full of fishing boats. In the early evening another yacht under Italian flag, a modern 26 foot folkboat built in fibreglass, pulled in and moored next to us, so we were two. We had a lot of fish and no refrigeration, so I divvied it up and gave the Italian boat some for their supper. Amicable relations all round.

The sirocco blew a furnace wind over us, a wind from the Sahara that deposited red Saharan sand everywhere. Over the time we sheltered from the sirocco we got to know the fishermen, Alfio the skipper, Charlie the main hand who was built like a Mr Universe with smouldering good looks to boot, and Palo, the young newbie. Alfio had worked in the Post Office in Messina and then had a minor stroke. He walked with a bit of a limp. After the stroke he got a small pension and decided to go sword-fishing to supplement his income.

When the sirocco died down Alfio asked if we wanted to go out fishing with them. So after the weather forecast in the early afternoon we hopped on the boat and set off out to sea. The boat was, I guess, around 35-38 feet, built of wood with the typically flared bows of Mediterranean fishing boats. There was virtually no navigation equipment apart from a VHF and a steering compass. I couldn't see a chart anywhere. Alfio headed directly out from Camerota until we were 10 or 12 miles off. Then the process of laying the long surface net began. The net is around 4 kilometres long and laid out by hand in a zigzag formation. Floating oil lamps were attached to the net every 200 metres or so. Alfio then laid a parachute sea anchor off the fishing boat at one end of the net and we lay down on the deck to sleep while one of the crew kept watch.

At 0300 in the morning we were woken and served little cups of double espresso rocket fuel. And then came the job of hauling the net in, all of it done by hand. I helped haul it in with Alfio and Charlie, always feeling the tension on the net for swordfish or tuna. We didn't want to 'unwrap' a swordfish or tuna Alfio explained, so when there was a bit of weight on the net it was hauled carefully keeping a good eye out for the fish in it. Soon a 10 foot swordfish plopped into the back of the boat, a good start to the catch.

Now I am pretty fit by this time, but the strength and fitness of Charlie and even the skinny Palo are something else. I have to stop and have a rest every 20 minutes or so. They just keep hauling the net in. We get a good catch, three good sized swordfish and a couple of tuna. I had been a little worried that I might be bad luck on the boat and, even worse, that Bridget, a woman on board, might throw any luck overboard and break every superstition these guys held on to. But the good catch has everyone in high spirits and Alfio gets me to drive the boat back while they all get some kip. Easier said than done.
What compass course shall I steer.
Alfio shrugs his shoulders.
See the cloud over there.
I see a puffy bit of morning cloud.
Head for that.
And so I do and Camerota comes up over the horizon. Don't ask me how.

We spend easy lazy days in Camerota. Every morning there is something on the deck to cook for supper. One morning there is an octopus lying on the deck and I have to ask Alfio what to do with it. He shows me how to tenderise it by bashing it on the quay and suggests I cut the legs up and make a stew with vegetables. It tastes OK but still a bit tough, probably because I didn't beat it enough on the quay. Alfio is trying to get me to go to Messina to get a new engine, a diesel, fitted.

You have a big heart but your engine has a small heart. Maybe no heart at all.

You come to Messina. We fit a diesel engine in your boat. This engine no good.

I don't have much money.

No problem. You come Messina. We fit engine.

We have been talking to the Italian boat next door and have decided to leave together for the Lipari Islands. Tomasio and his Swedish partner Helen are both psychiatrists with a yen for sailing. I drool over their folkboat, sturdily constructed in GRP, with a single cylinder diesel and electric start, an airy and spacious layout below, at least compared to *Roulette*, and everything so new and chunky shiny. She is also just so damnably pretty with sweet lines and a soft sheer as opposed to the reverse sheer of *Roulette*. I am proud of little *Roulette* and what she has been through, but I lust after this boat sitting next to me.

14-07-77 1430 Departed Camerota. Good wind. 3 knots speed.

We leave Camerota with hugs and a few tears. Alfio is still exhorting me to go to Messina. I tell him we will be OK and along with Tomasio and Helen leave for Stromboli in the Liparis. This is going to be an overnighter at 72 odd miles. The forecast looks fair and it's good to be on the way again. Tomasio has to put a reef in to slow down so we can keep up with him and together we sail across a smooth sea in a gentle Force 3. By evening the wind has dropped and Tomasio circles us suggesting he tow us. I decline and tell him we will catch him up at Stromboli or maybe Lipari, the main island. We are quite happy waiting for a breeze. Still Tomasio circles, becoming more and more insistent about giving us a tow. Eventually I relent and through the night and into the early morning we are towed towards Stromboli. In the early morning a breeze gets up and we let the tow go and sail towards the dull red glow of Stromboli, the lighthouse of the Mediterranean since ancient times. You can see the dull red of the eruptions for a good 20 miles off.

15-07-77 1330 Arrive off Stromboli. Anchored in deep water. Rolly.

Stromboli is a weird place. Here the local community really does live directly under a volcano spouting smoke and red hot lava that tumbles down the slopes on the other side of the island. You can hear the grumbling of the volcano and see the puffs of ash and smoke from the anchorage. We wander ashore into San Bartolomeo where there is a strange sense of calm and everyday normalcy to the place. Lots of the houses are decorated with frescoes and paintings of vines and flowers, with dolphins jumping out of the water, with almost hippy-esque primitive art-work. I can only guess that you just get used to living at the bottom of an active volcano and the rumbling and fire-spitting beast fades into background noise.

We trek up the slopes to the volcano. Under the hot sun it's hard work walking over rough scree and lumps of basalt. Eventually we get to the edge of the crater which booms and sends clouds of gas up, but we don't actually see any lumps of molten rock being blasted out and set off back to arrive at the anchorage before nightfall.

We leave the next day for Lipari in company with Tomasio and Helen. It was over dinner in Lipari that Tomasio explained why

I Roulette

they had been so determined to give us a tow.
Your friend Alfio told us that if we didn't look after you, tow you because your engine doesn't work very well, make sure you were all right, he would find us and ....

Tomasio drew his finger across his throat.

They are all mafiosa you know, those fishermen. I was scared.

I was embarrassed and apologised to Tomasio protesting that I knew nothing about this. Tomasio understood, but even so there was no way he was not going to tow us, just in case they found out.

Just down from the Lipari Island is Vulcano, another island with a simmering crater on it, though unlike Stromboli it rarely ejects molten lava. What it does do is warm the sea off it with geothermal vents and you swim around until you find just the right temperature between the vents. Some of the water is too hot to sit in. The sea bottom around the shores also has very fine mud which is said to be better than any commercial mud-pack you can buy. Everyone here coats themselves in this brown mud so it looks like a strange colony of aliens live here covered in gloopy brown stuff.

We sail down to Milazzo on Sicily with Tomasio and Helen, our last sail in company. They will leave the boat here until they get more time off later. Tomasio is worried about us going around the boot of Italy, but I reassure him that we will be OK. We have got this far. A last meal out and sad goodbyes. We all choose tuna baked in the oven with onion and peppers and cheese, a wonderful little feast of the palate, though Tomasio is wondering which fishing boat has caught it. Don't worry I say, Alfio is from Messina not Milazzo.

Scilla rears up from the sea just as Homer describes the lair of the sea monster Scilla. With six necks topped by dogs heads with razor sharp teeth, Scilla lived at the bottom of the rocky promontory that Scilla, the fishing village is built on, and would pluck unlucky sailors from their boats for a sea-monsterish snack. Odysseus knew of Scilla but still lost six of his men to her maws as they sailed past. There was a record of a whirlpool here until an earthquake in the 19th century altered the sea bottom and the whirlpool effectively disappeared. Across from Scilla in the Strait of Messina was Charybdis, another whirlpool that could suck small craft down to the bottom, so ancient mariners were literally between the twin dangers of Scilla and Charybdis. Go to close to one and the other would get you. I'm pretty happy we only have Charybdis to avoid.

10 Ionian

The Strait of Messina taking us down into the Ionian Sea looms like an iconic nautical barrier to *Roulette* getting down around the boot of Italy. This is the place that figures large in the *Odyssey* and if we had other ancient texts, was most likely on the minds of all ancient navigators. It has tides, running up to 4-5 knots at times. It has whirlpools that are really there and not some figment of ancient myth. It has overfalls and what the Italians wonderfully call 'bastardi', little whirlpools that suddenly appear and disappear. It has squalls and tricky winds. At either end of the strait it can be flat calm while in the strait it blows a hooley.

We set off from Scilla and avoided the Hydra-headed monster and Charybdis. In fact the short run down to Reggio di Calabria was a smooth relaxed affair that gave us a rather benign view of the Messina Strait. We pooh-poohed the ancients and their worries when in *Roulette* we could easily sail down at least as far as Reggio. The next day the weather looked fair for the 130 mile trip to Crotone tucked just inside the instep of the boot, or at least the start of the trip which I reckoned would entail at least two nights at sea.

20-07-77 1200 Left Reggio. Wind F 4-5.
Bumpy in Messina Strait.

Our earlier notions of the Strait of Messina were soon revised. We had bastardi and eddies and the tide taking us backwards for a while, all of it in a boisterous sea that kicked up spray all around us. OK you ancients, perhaps you had a clue or two about this place. By midnight we are only just out of the Messina Strait off Capo dell Armi after going backwards for a bit. *Roulette* is close hauled in a light easterly making around 2 knots, though at least the sea is quiet after the Messina Strait. From here we coast around the heel of the boot of Italy until we can strike off across to the inner sole and around the corner to Crotone.

It is quiet through the night without much wind so we make little progress. The log notes 2 miles made good for one 3 hour period in the early morning. By day-break we are doing a bit better at around 2 knots and it's looking like it will be a long haul to Crotone. By the afternoon the wind has picked up.

21-07-77   1500   4 knots. Good wind for Squillace.
Position off Capo Stilo marked.

Four knots on *Roulette* is flying and we revise our ETA to the 22nd. Somehow we are at ease with these speeds and in these seas in *Roulette*. It's not that we are not apprehensive about making these little voyages or that we are gung ho. It's a matter of quiet confidence, of working together to make it all happen, of sitting back and enjoying our snail-like passages under sail.

The nights out here are like nothing I have ever seen. The night sky is a cobalt blue canvas with a dense decoration of stars across it. Occasionally there is a 'fizzz' as a shooting star arcs over to the horizon. There are so many shooting stars we have run out of wishes and now just quietly contemplate them instead of shouting ooh and ahh, except if a really big one lights up the night sky. Years later I listened to an SSB conversation where Cheryl, a proper American dame, worried about what the Americans call 'falling stars'.
Oh my Gad. I mean, what would happen if say a star fell out of the Big Dipper, I mean, it wouldn't be the Big Dipper any more.

1 Roulette

I mean, like, all the constellations could change.
We were never entirely sure if Cheryl was for real or winding us up, but she kept us amused at nights on that long Atlantic passage.

22-07-77 0600 Arrive Crotone.
149 miles in 42 hours = 3.3 average speed.

We arrive at Crotone the next day at 0600. We tied up on the quay and both of us put our heads down for some sleep. At some time around midday my deep sleep is interrupted by someone stamping on the foredeck. I go up to find a band of pretty rough looking men motioning to me. I also notice the wind has got up and is blowing straight onto the quay. One of them speaks some English.
Quick. You must go over there. A storm is coming.
He points to the fishing boat quay on the other side.
OK. OK.
I need to start the engine. While I am down trying to get the engine started several of them have clumped on board and are untying ropes. We start drifting out and still that old Stuart Turner is reluctant to start. Eventually it does and one of them throws the kedge line off leaving the anchor on the bottom. I squeal a protest or two, but by now one of them is muscling me aside to take the tiller. I tell him in no uncertain terms that I will drive, though with a bit of a tremor in my voice. He is big and tough looking and could probably break some of my bones without a thought. Instead he laughs and agrees to let me drive and points to a fishing boat. We tie alongside and they jump off to attend to a large motorboat that is trying to berth nearby.

After half an hour they return.
You must give us something for saving your boat.

I shrug and indicate that we are a very small boat. And we don't have too much money. I go below and find a bottle of whisky. It's a bit of a mystery why we have it as neither of us are really whisky drinkers. I hand it to him.

OK. That's enough. Anyway the owner of the motorboat can pay for you. You are so small.

By this time it really is blowing onto the other quay so we are thankful we are here next to the fishing boat and being blown off rather than on. The two of us go below and Bridget makes tea while we both thank our lucky stars that we got off lightly from the local Mafia. I wonder what the owner of the motorboat is going to have to cough up. And then I remember my kedge is still on the bottom.

I run around to the quay that now has waves breaking on it and start to strip off. The Mafia guys are there and ask me what I am going to do.

Get the anchor.

No, no, no. You no do that.

Their mouths drop as I dive in. This is not an act of bravery, just a desperate attempt not to lose our kedge. Fortunately it is only 3 metres or so deep and I soon locate the rope and bring it to the surface. By this time there is a whole gaggle of them on the quay shouting at me. I get the rope to the quay and hand it up to one of them who pulls me up as well. We heave on the rope and eventually the anchor breaks free and we get it up on the quay. Bridget is there admonishing me when the head honcho sidles up.

This is for you he says, and with a grin hands the bottle of whisky back to me.

All is well in Crotone and I have the anchor and the whisky I don't drink.

Roulette

That evening we hear a hollah from the quay and there is Tomasio from the folkboat. He has been so worried about us that he has driven down from Rome to make sure we have arrived here safely. We hug him and tell him he is a silly old sausage for driving all that way, but secretly we are grateful for his care and fears for us. We have a brief drink and then he gets back into his car to drive all the way back to Rome. Bless him.

Crotone is a ramshackle place with crumbling buildings all around the waterfront. It doesn't even have much local life, a Calabrian spark that lights it up. Just the local Mafioso types who hang around the waterfront and who are now our friends. And yet we settle into the place and end up really liking it.

It was in Crotone that I realised just how small *Roulette* looked. As we were leaving some friends on a Swiss yacht took some pictures and when they gave them to us in Greece I realised that when I stood in the cockpit the coamings only came halfway up my calves. When you sat in the cockpit you can trail your hand in the water. It scared me a bit. I didn't make up some misty personal philosophy about being close to nature and old mother sea, more a slight worry about the frailty of this little ship.

I'm not sure why we elected to sail directly for Othoni, a little island off the northern end of Corfu. It's around 115 miles from Crotone whereas we could have stopped at Santa Maria di Leuca which is around 70 miles away. Still for whatever reasons we set a course directly for Greece.

25-07-77 1015 Good speed. Rough sea.
Roulette getting a good battering here.

The weather forecast looked good when we left Crotone, though the wind and sea we had seemed somewhat more than that forecast. Worse still we noticed the barometer had started to drop. I suspect the best thing to do would be to turn around and go back to Crotone. For some reason, perhaps a surfeit of confidence in our abilities, we decided to go on. We were doing a good speed and in the right direction.

Some 50 miles out we got a new forecast. A southerly gale was brewing in the Greek Ionian and was forecast to be blowing Force 7-8 in our sea area in 24 hours. What to do. I checked the charts and figured we could still make Othoni and find some shelter in a bay on the north side. We kept going.

26-07-77 0430 Horrid sea. 38 miles to Othoni.

One of the things we had brought back to the boat in France was a brand new storm jib in bright orange and made from that miraculous material terylene. It was time to get it out for only the second time and hank it on in place of the working jib. Normally I went up on the foredeck and changed the headsails. Bridget had been saying she should do it as well and so I let her climb up over the cabin and onto the heaving foredeck. What happened next is seared into my brain.

Roulette lurched on a wave and Bridget let go of the storm jib to hold on. The water over the deck picked up the storm jib and swept it over the side. Bridget looked at me in horror.
I'll dive in and get it.
No. NO. NO.
The idea of trying to turn around and get Bridget out of the water filled me with dread.
NO. Come back here. We'll keep the working jib up.

I Roulette

Bridget hesitated and then to my relief nodded her head as we both watched the sail float past. This was a scary moment and I still have visions of trying to haul Bridget out of the water and into the safety of *Roulette*. Thankfully this is just a nightmarish scenario that never happened.

By the time we were 5 miles off Othoni by my calculations and the island, which is quite high, had not hove into view, I was getting worried. Memories of the Channel crossing débâcle kept coming up and my brain was getting twitchy about our dead reckoning calculations. I checked and re-checked everything and Othoni should be there. A gale was imminent. Where was the bloody island?

It wasn't until we were less than 3 miles off that its shadowy outline appeared. The summer haze had obscured it from further out. Those ancient navigators must have experienced the same qualms as I did and the same relief when the landfall finally materialised. With the wind increasing all the time from the south we scouted the north side of the island until we found the bay. Thankfully the Stuart Turner fired up and we nosed into the bay, more of a bight really. In the clear water I could see there were big rocks, nay boulders, on the bottom and it took a while for us to potter around until we were happy we were in a sandy place. We laid two anchors out and watched the clouds scud off the top of the island. It was gusty in the anchorage, but relatively flat water, so we were happy. Just after we arrived a fishing boat motored into the bay and anchored off, ready to sit out the gale with us.

And we were in Greece.

11 Greece

The next afternoon the wind from the south had died and turned around to blow from the north. My doughty Denham, *The Ionian Islands to Rhodes*, mentioned an anchorage on the south side, so we sailed the short distance around the island to the hamlet of Othoni. There was a taverna and a general shop. The general shop catered for everything. We changed sterling for drachma. We bought a few supplies and had a beer in the taverna. And we wondered why on earth there was just us in *Roulette* and a Cigarette speedboat with three 100 HP outboards on the back.

It seemed no-one really wanted to tell us what the speedboat was doing there, but eventually a local fishermen told us it was a cigarette smuggling boat that had got caught up in the gale of the day before and had taken shelter here. We watched as jerrycans of petrol were loaded onto it and then at dusk the engines were fired up and off it went towards Italy. At speed.

A little later we discovered that this cigarette smuggling was a thriving little, or even quite big, business, in Ionian Greece. The cigarettes were picked up in Albania by small coasters. The tax on cigarettes in Hoxha's communist Albania was next to nothing. In Italy cigarettes are a government monopoly and the price was dictated by the government. The fast motorboats were based in Greece and joined up with the tramp steamers outside Greek territorial waters where they were hoisted on board and taken across to just outside Italian territorial waters. The fast motorboats were then loaded up with cigarettes which were run ashore on the Italian coast.

1 Roulette

From Othoni we make our way across to Corfu and around the coast to Corfu old town. The island is a landmark, something of a comma, in our travels. Greece was always the destination and you might expect that we were a bit lost now we had arrived. The sort of hollow feeling you get after sitting all your exams and passing. The pouring of effort and planning and industry into getting to a place that we have now arrived at. And yet it is not like that. We are excited to be here and the planning goes on for us to keep cruising around the coast and islands. And something else. A sea change that has come upon me more than it has for Bridget. I am slowly realising that I don't just like this life, I love all the logistics and the hopes and fears of voyaging from one place to another. I don't want to be in one place. I want to have a destination to sail to with all the landfalls and adventures along the way.

A few years after I arrived in Greece I came across Cavafy, the old Greek poet of Alexandria and his poem *Ithaca*. It captures this voyaging thing that had crept up on me in his lines.

Hope the voyage is a long one.
May there be many a summer morning when,
with what pleasure, what joy,
you come into harbours seen for the first time;
may you stop at Phoenician trading stations
to buy fine things,
mother of pearl and coral, amber and ebony,
sensual perfume of every kind —
as many sensual perfumes as you can;
and may you visit many Egyptian cities
to gather stores of knowledge from their scholars.

And here we are not that far from Ithaca. But not there yet.

This country breathes history through the very earth and rocks that it is composed of. It is a palimpsest of layers of history that have trammelled through it, that have built monuments which have been re-built by successive civilizations when the new has subdued the old, only to be subdued in turn by the new 'new'. The same sea and sky that we see, the same landfalls, the same winds and the same fears are all here.

My copy of the *Odyssey* is by now salt-stained and the glue in the binding has gone hard so I need to be careful when turning the pages. In Book V Homer relates how Odysseus gets from Calypso's island, most likely Malta, to Scheria, most likely Corfu.

Moreover, she made the wind fair and warm for him, and gladly did Ulysses spread his sail before it, while he sat and guided the raft skilfully by means of the rudder. He never closed his eyes, but kept them fixed on the Pleiades, on late-setting Bootes, and on the Bear- which men also call the wain, and which turns round and round where it is, facing Orion, and alone never dipping into the stream of Oceanus- for Calypso had told him to keep this to his left. Days seven and ten did he sail over the sea, and on the eighteenth the dim outlines of the mountains on the nearest part of the Phaeacian coast appeared, rising like a shield on the horizon.

This is all within the sea area we have just sailed in *Roulette*, well some of it anyway. It's around 350 miles from Malta to Corfu in a north-easterly direction. With westerlies, the prevailing wind in this area, he might have had trouble reaching Corfu on a raft. Still he had a sail and Calypso sends a warm wind, perhaps a southerly blowing off the Sahara. Telling him to keep the Pleiades and the Bear (Ursa Major) to his left works

1 Roulette

as these constellations give a good clue to where north is. So he is pointing in the right direction and making around 20 miles a day. He is on a raft after all and it gives a clue to how slow these voyages could have been. *Roulette* feels like something of a racehorse by comparison.

On *Roulette* we don't have a lot of room for books, but we do carry quite a lot of reference books and some of the classics as well as Denham's pilots and charts. Not that many charts but enough, touch wood, so far. There are odd books like Braudel's two volume *The Mediterranean and the Mediterranean World in the Age of Philip II*, something of a mouthful that puts many off, but these books are a mine of information on the Mediterranean. Classics like the *Odyssey* and Herodotus and a *Dictionary of Who's who in the Ancient World. Brewers Dictionary of Phrase and Fable.* And the *Shorter Oxford Dictionary*, how could anyone travel without it. These books are suffering from the salty atmosphere they are forced to live in and some of the bindings have been reinforced with brown parcel tape, but they help map out this world where you seem to be living half inside a mythological landscape and half in the modern world. Homer talks about the 'rosy fingered dawn' over the Pindus and there the Pindus range is, just over the water from us on mainland Greece. It's sort of spooky.

Mind you Corfu is not all Homer and the Phaeacians and gnarled ancient olive trees. Aircraft fly in low over the harbour bringing sun starved northerners to the tourist hotels around this coast. Shops in the old town sell awful tourist tat. The modern tourist world intrudes directly on the ancient landscape and it appears that these newcomers, the new 'new', want swimming pools and cheap beer and steak and chips more than they want any of the old stuff, of ancient stones and the ghosts

of Homer wandering around this ancient seascape. The guy in the yacht moored ahead of me encapsulates it all when he says What more could you want. Sun, sea and cheap beer.
Guess the ancients just passed him by.

While in Corfu old harbour we have a beautiful 35 footer next to us called *Rose Rambler*. Now if I had been up on current news of voyagers and their boats I would have recognised the boat and its owner. I had read Humphrey Barton's account of his Atlantic passages in *Vertue XXXV*, the 25 foot Vertue he proved could make successful ocean passages. I didn't know of his current boat *Rose Rambler*. We exchanged pleasantries and then one day he leaned over with a question.
Where would I get epoxy primer here?
Pretty sure you won't find it here. But it may just be your lucky day. I think I have a tin in the bilge.
Can I buy it off you?
Now that was tempting, but I figured after all the help I had had on the voyage down that it was my turn to help out. I gave him the tin which was leftover from epoxying *Roulette's* bottom in Dyers Boatyard and he handed it to Mary, his wife, who set about applying epoxy primer to the decks.
Shouldn't we give her a hand?
She will be fine. Come below for a drink.
So I sat below drinking with Humphrey Barton while Mary painted the decks. I was to see him off and on over the next few years. They would turn up in May after sailing across from Malta and potter around the Ionian until they headed back to Malta in September. Humphrey was a sailor of the old school. In an anchorage off Argostoli on Cephalonia *Rose Rambler* came slowly into the bay.
What depth are you in Rod?
Oh, around 4 to 5 metres, it's all deep enough.

I Roulette

Metres eh?

On another occasion I was on board for a drink congratulating him on winning the Blue Water Medal from the Cruising Club of America.

Show him the telegram you sent back when they suggested you come to collect it in July, urged Mary. Humph rummaged around and produced his telegram which read: 'July is no month to be crossing the Atlantic'. His dry wit and laconic presentation were a delight.

We take our leave of this place with a bitter-sweet feeling of awe and regret to head down to the island of Paxos. There is very little wind off the coast of Corfu and the sun burns down on us so we decide a swim is in order. I trail a line out the back and Bridget dives in first. I follow. Although *Roulette* hardly appears to be moving it's surprising how hard it is to keep up with her. We decide this lark is a bit silly and we would both look really silly if *Roulette* sailed off leaving us splashing around naked in the Corfu Channel. We climb back on board and as we do I notice a slick off the back of the boat. Then a black dorsal fin cuts the surface and a shark, maybe six foot long, swims past *Roulette*. Now that would have been really silly floating naked around the Corfu Channel with a shark.

The wind soon picks up from the north and we tootle off down to Gaios on Paxos. The small town, really a large village, is tucked behind an islet and you don't see it until you are in the channel between the islet and the larger island and turn the corner where the waterfront reveals itself. I have a little trouble berthing bows-to on the quay when the kedge line gets caught, so I give the throttle a bit of a nudge. The kedge line frees itself, but the throttle is stuck half open and we accelerate towards the quay despite my pulling on the kedge line with all my might. I manage to reach over and turn the petrol tap off but not before Bridget has leapt ashore to act as a human fender and is yelling at me to stop the engine. Eventually the carburettor empties itself and the Stuart Turner is silent.

We attract a small audience for our performance and go off for a drink with some of them. They are part of a flotilla, Flotilla Sailing Club, and are on their way back up to Corfu. The boats are a mixture of Jaguar 27's and lifting keel Jaguar 22's and the skipper is Martin Evans and his sister Sue. This chance meeting will shape my life in the years to come in ways I would never have predicted.

We potter south through the Ionian, to Preveza and then on and down the canal to Levkas town. It's getting late in the season and we need to find somewhere to lay *Roulette* up and go back to England to work. We are living on around £2.50 a day and that means a lot of basic rice dishes and very little life ashore.

Opposite Levkas town is a boatyard on the far bank of the canal and we row across to negotiate hauling for the winter. Christo who runs it is a jovial character built like a barrel and with forearms nearly as thick as my calves. He tells us not to worry about money, we will sort it out when we come back, and just to turn up and he will sledge us out of the water. I press him for a price, but he is adamant he will see us right on our return.

This Greek system of favours takes a bit of getting used to. It's like you fill up the metaphorical cookie jar and then there will be a light conversation over a glass or two when the owner of the cookie jar wants a cookie or two. No set prices. Really just a matter of cookies going from one jar to another, some of the jars more full than others. We are used to price tags on everything and contracts stipulating the terms and conditions, so getting used to the cookie jar system goes against the hard price-tag system and the way we are used to doing business. There is a looseness to it that is outside my range of experience.

Under Levkas is the area called the inland sea where the outer islands form a barrier to any big swell entering and inside the sea is peppered with islands to sail to. We motor off down the canal and head for Nidri and what Denham calls Tranquil Bay opposite. Here we bump into Martin on the flotilla again and a fortuitous offer to help out and importantly get paid. The mixture of Jaguar 27's and 22's is not really working out. The Jaguar 22's only have outboards to propel them and can't keep up with the bigger Jaguars. So we are to be in charge of the 22's, around five of them, and to help out cleaning boats and getting them ready for turnaround when new customers arrive. And we get £100 a week for the two of us, a fortune and the answer to our dwindling funds.

We sail back up to Levkas and leave *Roulette* there under the kindly eye of Christo and move onto one of the Jaguar 22's. It seems huge compared to *Roulette* and so well equipped. True the outboard is pretty useless when it comes to motor-sailing in a chop as it keeps lifting clear of the water and sounds like an electric mixer until the stern settles back in and the outboard grunts with the effort of pushing water again. That doesn't bother us as we are pretty used to slow passages in *Roulette* anyway and feel grateful when the engine starts. Down below there is a galley and a double in the forepeak. The large main hatch lifts up with canvas sides so there is standing headroom in the galley area. Standing headroom, even a little, is the acme of luxury as far as we are concerned.

We follow Martin's flotilla around and everything goes tickety-boo. We clean up the boats after a two week flotilla and meet and greet the new arrivals. I'm still pinching myself that we are actually getting paid to sail around this area. Yacht charter is in its infancy here and Flotilla Sailing Club are really the only charter company. Everywhere we go we are greeted by taverna owners who can't believe that a whole gaggle of boats have turned up with 40 or so potential customers.

The season ended in late September and the promise of a job with Flotilla Sailing Club the next year as full blown skipper and hostess. Escorting the Jaguar 22's around the Ionian had been great fun, but in lots of ways it was good to get back to *Roulette* and given our new found addition to funds, we decided we should do a bit more sailing around the area before laying up in Christo's boatyard.

There is something here that I only vaguely recognise at this time. Doing the charter thing has been fun and topped up the kitty, but it leaves some spiritual gap to do with taking your own little craft on a voyage from A to Z. The planning, the poring over charts, the joy of new landfalls and even the hard stuff beating to windward to get to an island anchorage that seems so far off, I miss all that. And it has come as something of a surprise.

We had loosely talked about selling *Roulette* in Greece and then returning to New Zealand to continue with earning a living there. I have shipped all my stuff back to NZ, all my books and papers and other junk. Now I'm not so sure. It's an indeterminate feeling, a bit of a mystery, a slight niggle that I brush off with a 'well, we will return the year after'. Bridget is less sure about staying on here next year. She is not homesick, just not sure about continuing this sea gypsy story where we sail around with a small budget but lots of freedom, whatever that freedom means. It's an unexpected turn to my life and not one I had really planned.

We sailed down into the Gulf of Patras and on to Galaxidhi in the Gulf of Corinth. There was no-one else sailing around and it all seemed so wild and unexplored, though my Denham told me that was not so. It didn't really matter because it seemed so. In Galaxidhi it was time to sail back to Levkas and haul *Roulette*. At least now it seemed like a comma in the proceedings and not the end of something that had fired my imagination and held the promise of working on yachts out here in the next year. Little accidents of fate, a little crack in the heavens that lets the light in, such small things that shape and twist who we are and what we do, now that seems like the old gods at work.

12 Coda

There is a little more to this story of sailing down to Greece in *Roulette* than I have mentioned here. I need to come clean about one of the underlying causes of this voyage down to the lands of myth and reason in a small yacht that probably shouldn't have left the sheltered waters of the Solent. In 1974 when I was 25 years old my world was shattered when I was diagnosed with an aggressive cancer. I had a malignant melanoma and the prospects didn't look good.

The surgeons duly chopped a pound of flesh out of my back in an elliptical fillet and then proceeded to chop out bits of lymph glands. The prognosis was not good. New Zealand has one of the highest incidents of skin cancer in the world and even in those early days knowledge of the disease was well advanced. It didn't take much research on my part in the university library and talking to friends in medical school to work out that two years was the normal allotted span. For some reason a warped male nurse in the hospital had suggested as much when he said We will see you back here in two years. We always do.
Nor did it help when I heard a more-pork call in the daytime as I walked out of the hospital. Maori folklore has it that if you hear a more-pork, the little native owl of NZ, call in the daytime then a death is foretold.

I never did go back to the hospital out of some stubborn resolve to at least see something of the world while I could. It took a little while to pack up life in Auckland and then with Bridget we embarked on the *Angelina Lauro*, on its last voyage to Europe as a cruise ship before it was retired to Chile to work as a ferry. We didn't especially want to go on a cruise ship, but it was cheaper in those days to take cheap berths on the

I Roulette

Angelino Lauro compared to flying. And so we zig-zagged our way across the Pacific and the Atlantic to Genoa.

My diagnosis was in a fundamental way the spark that got me started on the idea of a voyage down to the Mediterranean in a small boat. This was not seen as some cataclysmic end to it all or some weepy sort of moment. It was more like a nagging toothache that popped up at odd times and tempered my perception of the world. I wanted to see something of this old Europe, of places I had read about, of cultures I knew next to nothing of, the peoples around the shores of the Mediterranean. At the time it appeared I had limited amounts of that elusive stuff 'time' to do this. That I chose a boat called *Roulette* to embark on this adventure may have been fate, I prefer serendipity. But was I making the right call?

As it turned out I called it right. I've lasted longer than those two years, a span that seems so small from this great height, a treasured amount of borrowed time. I might still be in New Zealand working in some job or other, wishing I was somewhere else and maybe, just maybe, dreaming of that old Europe and the Mediterranean so far away. The result of this brush with mortality lead to years of sailing the Mediterranean and writing yachting guides to many of the countries around it. It's a mystery as most of the best of life is.

We worked for a few years on flotilla though not with Flotilla Sailing Club. At the Boat Show I was poached by a company that was setting up a new flotilla operation. Crawford Perry Travel ran a skiing operation and had decided to start up a summer sailing programme: CPT Cruising in Greece. I was taken on to help buy the boats, equip them, and get them down to Greece. More by luck than sound judgement we bought

Cobra 850's built in Waterlooville, the equipment to go on them and had them trucked to Brindisi. Here crew, largely from British Airways, sailed them across to Spetses in the Saronic where we were to be based. I had never been there before.

Roulette was equipped with a new terylene mainsail and other new gear and sold to Gadi Katz, a giant Israeli who wanted to sail around the Mediterranean. How he fitted in the boat I have no idea, but he cut his teeth sailing *Roulette* and then moved on to other boats.

In 1980 I set off to do the research and write *Greek Waters Pilot*, a project that proved to be somewhat bigger and more difficult than I had imagined and a project which would lead me off in unimagined directions. Oh, and I had all my stuff in NZ shipped back to Europe.

I Roulette

Roulette in Dyers Boatyard on the Itchen

Bridget in the cosy confines of *Roulette*

Moving over to let a peniche through on the Canal Lateral a Garonne

Roulette sailing in the Mediterranean

Alfio mending the nets as we head out of Camerota for a night's fishing

With Tomasio and Helen in *Milazzo*

Roulette on her last trip in the Saronic before she was sold in the winter of 1977-1978

Hauled out in Christo's Boatyard in Levkas

II Rozinante

1985 & 1987

An account of taking a Mirror Offshore 18 down the Danube through the Iron Curtain countries to the Black Sea and then on to Istanbul and down the Turkish Aegean coast to Bodrum. This account describes the eastern bloc before the 'Velvet Revolution' that swept away the old Soviet dominance and changed the face of Mitteleuropa and eastern Europe and many of the geographical boundaries as well. I have kept the old country names and boundaries from 1987.

There was a great difference in boats, of course. For a long time I was on a boat that was so slow we used to forget what year it was we left port in.
Mark Twain, Life on the Mississippi

1   1985   On foot down the Danube

It's a bit of a mystery how my fascination with this river started. For starters it's a river and my medium is the open sea. Maybe I read something about the Danube in a newspaper or magazine or perhaps someone mentioned the Danube in conversation. More likely I was contemplating alternative routes to the Mediterranean over the Biscay or French canal routes. Whatever it was I started doing some research and things got out of hand. Before long I had acquired a substantial library on the Danube and even gone so far as to get the huge volumes of the Danube pilots covering the lower Danube, from the Danube Commission in Budapest. These are beautiful and detailed and cost a small fortune. It seemed this river winding its way from the Black Forest to the Danube Delta in Romania had cast some sort of spell on me.

The Danube is the only major river running from west to east in Europe. It winds its way from Germany down to the Black Sea in Romania. Most of the countries it passes through are in the Eastern bloc on the other side of the Iron Curtain, a name that conceals more than it reveals. Somehow the term 'Iron Curtain' intimates a group of homogeneous countries under communist rule, the outlying satellites of the Soviet Union. It allows little of the individual culture and history of the different countries, as I was to find out.

Just before I left for the Danube a letter dropped through the postbox to tell me my father had died in New Zealand. My father had left my mother when I was nine and I had seen him on only a few occasions since that time, but memories are still strong of his stories of North Africa and Italy in WWII, of hunting and fishing in remote Tokomaru Bay on the East Cape of New Zealand, I guess of a father figure. I can still see the faded black and white photos of the war, still feel that hand guiding mine to steer the tractor on the farm, of the all to brief time when he was a father figure in my life. So I leave for the Danube with a strange sense of loss, though the loss is a patchy picture that swims in and out of my consciousness always touching on the brevity of this life and the need to get on with this little adventure.

In 1985 I made my first trip down the Danube. Without a plan, but with a substantial amount of research on the Danube rattling around my head, I set off in June and took a ferry to Zeebrugge and a train to Donaueschingen at the source of the Danube in the Black Forest. The Danube here is a relative trickle and has nothing about it of the mighty river it becomes.

I've reverted to being a backpacker for this trip. The usual law of backpacking applies: pack the minimum and then take it all out and pack half of that. So I had the minimum for the trip with a few clothes and a very slim sleeping bag that rolled up into nothing. I planned to stay in pensions or small hotels most of the way and omitting tent, stove and all that stuff meant I had more room for a small collection of useful reference and other books on Mitteleuropa. And a small German-English phrasebook because German is the common language of the river. I do feel a bit like the oldest backpacker on the river, but I'm sure I'll get over that.

The valley that the Danube follows rolls gently downhill making it the logical place to build the railway line that runs along this stretch of the Danube. I took the local train, it has just two carriages, to Ulm. The river here has lots of shallows and is not navigable for anything other than rowing boats and small motorboats. It is shaded by trees with fields sloping gently down to it and then cuts through little gorges with turreted Schloss built on the top.

Up until the 18th century Ulm was the uppermost terminal for going down the Danube in what were called 'Ulm boxes'. There is a replica of one at Ulm and it really is nothing more than a box, a flat-bottomed barge with steering oars at either end. The boxes were loaded with cargo and passengers at Ulm and then drifted downstream controlled as best they could be by the steering oars. A rowing boat was carried to take lines ashore so that the barge could be controlled through rapid sections of the river. Presumably the boxes were broken up at their destination since there was no way they could get back upstream. They fell out of use when steam and later the diesel engine arrived on the scene.

From Ulm the train continues on down to Regensburg, the upper reach of the navigable Danube in the 20th century. The huge commercial docks downriver from Regensburg proper are home to the 1000 ton barges using pushing or towing tugs to bring trains of barges up and down river. This is also the place where the Rhine-Main-Danube Canal will join the navigable Danube to the Baltic and northern Europe. (Completed 1992).

A ferry runs down to Passau from here once a week and I bought a ticket and was soon afloat on the river heading downstream for the German-Austrian border. This was the way the river should be experienced, afloat on it and working the currents, checking the navigable channel and lining up for the locks on the way. Well at least I assumed that was what the skipper of the ferry did. The ferry stops at various villages along the way, a bit like the local train or bus and locals have obviously been visiting friends, doing a bit of shopping in Regensburg and then catching the ferry back home. There are quite a few locks on this upper section to tame the river so barge traffic can get up and down safely. These are huge locks, big enough to fit several lighters in and dwarfing our ferry.

At Passau I knew a ferry ran down to Vienna leaving early in the morning, so I found a sheltered nook near the docks and slept outside for the night. The ferry down to Vienna is a sizeable beast and makes just a few stops along the way. Like the ferry from Regensburg it mostly seems to be used by locals, some of them in lederhosen and humping accordions along for a bit of impromptu music on the trip.

The ferry arrived late in Vienna and I hurried off to find a hotel. Between the old course of the river and the new there is an island where the ferry stops and a short walk across the island soon found me in a street of hotels that looked affordable. The receptionist eyed me strangely when I asked for a room, but took my money and showed me to a small room that was clean and had a view over the street.

As I unpacked I noticed there seemed to be a fair amount of coming and going in the hotel and on the street outside a number of elegantly dressed young women hovered on the pavement. Light-bulb flashes and tired man from the Vienna ferry realises he is in a hotel used by the ladies of the night. Still it was relatively cheap for Vienna and once the ladies realised I wasn't a customer they were friendly and often plied me with chocolates and fancy cakes, presents from satisfied customers no doubt.

I spent a week in Vienna trying to organise a berth on a barge train going downriver. A couple of times I thought I had succeeded only for the ride to fall through. In the end I figured I would have to go by cruise boat from Budapest. Between Vienna and Budapest a hydrofoil runs every day and so I said goodbye to the girls in the hotel and hopped on the hydrofoil down to Budapest.

The cruise boat, the *Oltenita,* under Romanian flag, was sitting on the dock in Budapest. It was mostly populated by pensioners 'doing' the Danube and we were all escorted by our Romanian guide, the portly Maria. I guess someone must have seen me scribbling surreptitiously, or so I thought, in a notebook, or asking questions that the normal river tourists didn't ask, but somehow they found out I was writing a book or involved with something like that, something not quite kosher for the Romanians. I had listed my occupation as 'teacher' on the various forms I had to fill out before joining the boat. Not that their information was perfect when on the first night Maria welcomed us on board and announced to the assembled group that she would especially like to welcome the three South African journalists. The retired South African couple next to me expressed surprise to Maria and I sort of stuttered a vague denial, not least the fact I wasn't South African.

The *Oltenita* wended its way down the Danube through Hungary and into Yugoslavia. It stopped at a few places along the way, at Vukovar in Yugoslavia, Belgrade, and then Turnu Severin in Transylvania, the home of Dracula or more accurately Vlad the Impaler. This was all interesting in a sanitised sort of way. There were only organised excursions ashore and the chance of meeting your everyday Hungarian or Croat or Serb or Romanian was scant. Something was missing and I felt cheated, though what did I really expect anyway on a cruise boat on the Danube? Just a bit more I guess.

Maria took me under her wing and by the time we got to Romania was lecturing me on the social works of the leader, the great and benevolent father of the nation, Nicolae Ceausescu. She showed me apartment blocks built for the workers, hospitals and schools, roads and motorways. In every way, Maria told me, implored to me, he had made life better. I must have been muted in my response because one night she burst into tears and begged me to write nothing but good about the country. It seemed she was really quite fearful of her masters in case she hadn't done her job properly.

In Cernavoda at the end of the cruise I took an excursion to a small hotel in the Danube delta. The locals fished for sturgeon roe, caviare, in tar black rowing boats they took through the narrow reed-lined channels. I managed to wangle my way onto one and along with a police boat accompanying us, our little flotilla of boats wound its way through the delta. I was a little surprised when we met up with some Bulgarian boats and Bulgarian wine and sausages were swapped for Romanian caviare. I asked one of the grizzled fishermen how they got away with it right in front of the police boat. He looked at me and then said that in this lonely place somewhere in the delta, well... and he drew his hand across his throat.
They have to live here with us you know.

The day before I left, my room had been searched. Everything was neatly put back in its place, but not quite in its place. Fortunately I had my notebooks with me, but I was getting a little paranoid about the Securitate, Ceausescu's secret police, which have a reputation for carelessness with human life.

Romania is a country where even typewriters had to be registered.

I left for Bucharest and breathed a sigh of relief when my train headed south over the river and into Bulgaria on its way to Istanbul. Still this initial trip on foot was not enough. I felt that I needed to explore the Danube in a boat of some sort. There needed to be more intimacy with the people and the countries along the way, more intimacy with this river itself, some nitty-gritty and more visceral experience of this big old river cutting Europe into two.

2 1987 ROZINANTE

I needed a boat and it needed to be cheap. It also needed a diesel engine for the river. I searched the 'boats for sale' in various sailing magazines and revised my ideas of a nice 25 footer about 10 years old downwards. Finally I found a Mirror Offshore 18 or 19, I was never sure as the paperwork mentioned both numbers. It was owned by a sound engineer from the BBC, though he evidently hadn't used it often. I pretty much worked out it had sat neglected on the Thames at Twickenham for a few years. What I didn't work out was that at some stage she had also sunk on her mooring.

The Mirror Offshore was designed by Van de Stadt for a competition run by The Mirror newspaper group. Hence the name. The brief was for a small motor-sailor that was affordable by 'the average' man. The result was a tubby little boat measuring a tad under 19 feet long and a beam of 6.75 feet, somewhat beamier than *Roulette*, the 20 foot ply boat I had sailed down to the Mediterranean. It had triple keels with a long central keel and bilge keels and drew under 2 foot.

Inside was a miniature heads on the starboard side that you needed to fold yourself into and even then it was next to impossible to close the door. To port was a single burner cooker and a bit of stowage. From there a berth extended right up to the forepeak and back again on the other side. This was a curious arrangement as it was only long enough to sleep one on either side with space left over at the ends. Unless you are very short. It came with a Volvo MDI rated around 8 HP and it seemed to run OK after a quick service.

There is no way you could say *Rozinante* was a beautiful boat. Tubby with high cabin sides, she looked a bit like a bath toy made large. But inside the skin of the tubby little boat there was a stocky work horse trying to get out, or at least so I hoped when I named her *Rozinante* after Don Quixote's nag, an old farm horse that he thought was superior to thoroughbreds. I could see definite parallels between the boat I had just bought and my view of what it could and would do. *Rozinante* came with two bright red plastic sails, the mainsail and a hanked on working jib. I'm not sure whether this was some special sort of plastic, terylene it was not, but the sails had seen little use and though I worried about their durability, that proved not to be a problem by the end of the voyage.

The other problem I had was how to get *Rozinante* down to Regensburg. I rang up several yacht haulage companies and got quotes that ranged from £2000 and up to transport my little ship to Regensburg. The Rhine-Main-Danube Canal was not finished at this time so I figured trucking it down would be a logical move. Not at that price. I bought an old Rover 3½ litre V8 and found I could hire a big flat-bed trailer. All in car and trailer came in at around £1000 and I planned to sell the Rover when it came back to England. It was a project sired on a shoe-string and running on a lot of hope, but it seemed perfectly feasible.

Now all I needed was crew. Bridget, my old partner on *Roulette*, had been working for a charter company in the Caribbean and was at a bit of a loose end. I put it to her that this would be an interesting adventure, no commitments or close quarters stuff, just two friends on an adventure. A friend, Graham, tired of telephones and too many business lunches, agreed to take time off to help us get *Rozinante* to the Danube

II Rozinante

and to do his best to drive the ailing Rover back to England where he would return the trailer to the hire company and put the car up for sale. Odile, a French friend, wanted to come out for a couple of weeks later in the trip. It was to prove an interesting cocktail of interpersonal relations.

Just before we left Graham procured an old Johnson 20 HP outboard. *Rozinante* had a bracket on the back, though I thought the big old 20 HP would likely bring the bow right out of the water and maybe flip her over. I managed to swap it for a 4 HP that looked more the job than the big outboard. We were also a bit light on safety gear and navigation equipment. There were a couple of kapok life-jackets and I bought a couple of flares. We had a steering compass of sorts mounted on the bulkhead, a hand-bearing compass and an echo-sounder, the old type with a red light that whizzed around giving a solid red line to give depth. And I had a good supply of charts for the Danube, the Black Sea, the Sea of Marmara and the Aegean. I was hopeful it would all turn out all right. Bridget was less happy with the equipment and suggested, quite forcibly, that I buy some more flares, a couple of decent life jackets and a rudimentary first aid kit.

16th June   The alarm clock went off at 0630. Time to drive through London's traffic clogged streets to pick up the hired flat-bed trailer in St Albans. The old Rover fires up and we, me and Bridget, rattle off around the North Circular to St Albans. The owner of the hire company is a bit worried about what we are going to transport on the twin-wheeled trailer and rattles off a list of do's and don't's. Don't curb the wheels or it will cost you. Don't load any more than 3 tons on the trailer. And what I am transporting. I tell him we are loading a small boat on it. I don't tell him we are driving down to Germany.

Eventually we get away and drive down to Toughs boatyard in Teddington where I had left *Rozinante* the previous day. She is soon craned onto the trailer and fastened down with some truck strops. With triple keels she is quite stable on the trailer, but the old Rover wheezes a bit now there is a ton or more of weight on the trailer.

I drive back to Tooting in South London where all the supplies are loaded on. On the lower Danube it will be difficult getting food in some parts of Bulgaria and most parts of Romania, so I have bought enough provisions to see us through this whole stretch of the river. *Rozinante* looks so odd parked on the street in South London and passers-by keep stopping and looking at her parked in front of the flat. Neighbours are curious.
Where are you going?
The Danube river.
Where's that?
It starts in Germany and runs down to the Black Sea.
I'd elaborate further, but there are glazed looks and a few 'good lucks' and mostly incomprehension.

17th June   The last minute essentials are packed: black pepper and garlic, sellotape and a pencil sharpener, exhaust repair bandage and spare oil. I've assembled tea bags and coffee. Olive oil and rice and pasta. Magazines are treasured in Bulgaria and Romania so I have copies of *Scientific American*, *Time* and *Newsweek*, *Elle* and *Vogue*, and a few yachting magazines for comfort. Graham arrives at 1730 and we're off to Dover for the 2330 ferry to Zeebrugge. The trailer wheels are splayed out with the weight of the boat and equipment and provisions, the transmission whines in protest somewhere in the bowels of the Rover, but we are off. No fanfares. No bon voyage. Just us and *Rozinante*.

II *Rozinante*

We make it to Dover, but nearly don't make it onto the ferry. I pray as the transmission whines and squeals and there is a nasty smell of burning transmission fluid. Bit by bit we make it onto the ferry to Zeebrugge. Thankfully it will be downhill to get off.

18th June 0600. Trundling along at 50 mph in Belgium. After a coffee and croissant stop life seems good. The sun comes up over the countryside and I have to pinch myself that, so far, so far, things seem to be humming. At 1200 we cross into Germany at Aachen and customs don't even bother to ask about *Rozinante* perched proudly on the trailer behind us.

The Rover trundles on through the day, though we do need to keep the heater on full with the windows down to stop it overheating. We stop for the night at a farm gasthaus in the middle of nowhere. Dinner is 'what he has' which turns out to be fresh asparagus, home cured ham sliced thick, boiled potatoes and steins of good beer. Germany is growing on me.

3 Germany

19th June   We arrived in Regensburg at dusk and headed for the docks with a skyline of cranes apparently offering unlimited opportunities to put the boat in the water. It took a kind guard at one of the dock gates to direct us to the Regensburg Motorboot Club on the other side of the river where, he thought, we might find a crane more suited to our purpose. As I drove down the narrow lane to the club a car coming the other way flashed its lights at us and pulled over. When we stopped the driver got out.

Hi. I'm Joe. You want the boat in the water. I do it tomorrow. 8.30 OK. Right. You follow me to the club now.
I couldn't get a word in edgeways and was in any case too surprised by the rapid-fire offers that tumbled out of Joe in a thick German-American accent. At the club Joe continued in the same vein.
You park here. I'm gonna put you in the water for sure tomorrow morning. We got toilets here. We gotta kitchen in the clubhouse. We got cold beer in the machine there at one deutschmark. White beer, black beer. I don't think you'll like white beer. What the hell. What you like.

Bridget and I slept in *Rozinante* on the back of the trailer for the night while Graham opted for the back seat of the Rover.

20th June   In the morning Joe was as good as his word. German punctuality. In fifteen minutes we were in the water and tied up alongside a pontoon at the club. However, Joe did warn us that the water level was three metres above the norm for the time of year and that we should wait until it went down. It would only take a couple of days to drop two metres, he reckoned - as long as it didn't rain any harder. It seemed impossible to us that the level could drop 2 metres in a couple of days. Graham and I arranged a system of stick markers on the club steps that normally went down to the water's edge and reckoned that when the level got to the second step from the bottom, it was time to go.

We occupied our time touring the surrounding countryside and exploring Regensburg. On one of our trips we came across a festival complete with whole roast pig, roast chicken and big buxom women who somehow carried three steins of beer in each hand. We ate, even Bridget the vegetarian demolished half a roast chicken, and drank deeply.

I found myself sitting next to a voluble and strange man in his 40's who extolled the virtues of Bavaria and of shooting because, as it happened, this festival was largely devoted to some Bavarian gun club or other. And our friend was evidently a good shot. His name was called out and the host handed him a high-powered rifle complete with telescopic sights, a prize for overall shooter of the year. He proudly handed it to me when he sat back down and a little hesitantly I examined this bit of armoury that would likely stop a wild boar at half a mile.

23rd June   After three days, as Joe and the club members had prophesied, the level of the water was down to the second step, a good two metres. The medieval bridge just downstream was the first obstacle. It has only two navigable arches, one for going upstream and one for down. As with a lot of things, fear hardly entered into shooting the medieval bridge. I barely had time to line the boat up and gun the small diesel up to full revs before *Rozinante* was sucked through the arch and spat out the other side into a standing wave that covered the boat in spray.

Graham was on the downstream side taking photographs of the event and after picking him up, I asked him what it had looked like. I wanted someone to tell me how grand it had looked as all nineteen foot of *Rozinante* was belched through the arch by the Danube.

Two white faces in a blue boat covered with spray through a shaking viewfinder. He was more nervous about the whole thing than we had been and the photographs subsequently showed this - they were so blurred from camera shake that none of them were usable. But he added that the good burghers of Regensburg had looked suitably amazed at the feat and I nursed a picture of their surprised faces for the next thirty kilometres.

The Danube runs with a fair amount of current in this section. The kilometre posts along the banks make it easy to time how long a kilometre is taking and in the full force of the current *Rozinante* was doing a good 11-13 kilometres an hour, 6-7 knots, with the engine on tick-over to give steerage way. We watch the posts flash by the Bavarian countryside. Much of the river is forested along its banks, silver birch and elm and reeds, a sombre landscape in a misty rain that is almost like a blurred water colour of how you would imagine a riverscape in the middle of Europe.

After nearly sixty kilometres, which didn't take long with all that current whooshing us downriver, a half-moon bridge and street-lights appeared through the rain-driven dusk. This was the lock just before Straubing. The lock-keeper let us into the lock and *Rozinante* looked plain silly tucked into the corner alongside the huge concrete wall. If you blinked you would miss her. The lock-keeper looked bemused, but locked us through.

II *Rozinante*

In Straubing we tied alongside the ferry pontoon and rigged the cockpit tent just before the sky dumped buckets of rain on Straubing. Our only problem here was where the three of us would sleep with the rain heaving down. Eventually we put some of the forepeak cushions and a sleeping bag on the cabin sole and three of us were able to sleep snugly out of the rain. Though you couldn't get up in the night for a pee.

24th June   In the morning we shopped between rain showers and when *Rozinante* left Straubing we were stocked for a siege. Part of this was a continuous bolstering of the provisions for Bulgaria and Romania. We stopped for lunch in Deggendorf. Squat Soviet-beige ships, smartly painted but ugly craft, loaded ore at the commercial port across the river. They are more like small ocean-going ships than barges except the superstructure is kept low so they can pass under bridges on the river.

Downstream of Deggendorf I spotted a little harbour at Hofkirchen. The technique for getting into these places was to turn *Rozinante* around into the current and throttle up while edging across to the side of the river. You could usually spot the counter-current near the bank of the river and when *Rozinante* had edged close enough and hit the counter-current she would suddenly surge forward and I'd need to throttle back. There was somewhat more control than it appeared, though once inside the little harbour I'd need to throttle right back or even go astern.

Rozinante drawing something under 2 foot could snuggle into these tiny harbours that mainly had small motorboats in them. In Hofkirchen one of the locals helped us tie up and welcomed us to Bavaria. On the subject of somewhere to eat he indicated there was a gasthaus in the village that served food.

We washed and preened and prepared for a night out. Graham had to leave tomorrow from Passau so we thought a good meal was in order before he left. We wandered along the bank of the Danube in the evening light heading for the spire of the large church. We found the gasthaus and sat down for a drink. The owners sons, huge blond Aryan youth, served us steins of beer and translated what was on the menu. Bavarians are big eaters and large plates of food arrived with more beer and good cheer with our hosts. We almost felt Bavarian if we had been tall and fair enough.

After dinner Graham announced that he wanted local liqueur. After Graham I emptied the shot glass in one and then both of us stared at each other.

Did you feel that?

Somehow you felt the liqueur go down and then come tingling back up your spine to the brain. We had to have another one to make sure. The Aryan giant sat down next to me and smiled.

This is Bavarian schnapps. It's made from a secret recipe, from a root found only deep in the forest. You know, Mandrake root. He scribbled the shape of a knobbly root in the shape of a man on the paper napkin. This was weird. The blond giant then motioned to me.

You come to see our shooting range.
Sorry, can you say that again. Where is it?

I motioned to Graham who nodded his head in disbelief. Bridget decided she would come as well. The giant led us to a big trap-door in the floor, opened it, and down we went into a huge underground cellar. There on one side was the shooting range. Targets were automatically returned on a pulley system and a selection of .22 rifles was lined up in front.

You want a go.
Sure.

Now in my somewhat inebriated state giving me a .22 rifle was just plain silly. Still I felt the balance of it, aimed and fired. The damned thing had a hair trigger. My first shot was OK, but subsequent shots got worse. The blond giant picked his rifle up and peppered the area around the bulls-eye. Bavaria 10. Boatman 2. I was just glad I hadn't been fighting his grandfather in the war.

25th June   Graham had to leave us at Passau to get the train back to Regensburg and drive the ailing Rover and the hired trailer back to England. I turned *Rozinante* into the current near a likely quay at Passau and we tied up. A man in a uniform wandered along to tell us a ferry was due in soon. We moved to another vacant space to be told the same thing. Finally we found a space tucked in under the stern of a barge and things looked hopeful. Until a policeman strode up to us and like an imperious traffic warden told us if we didn't move in five minutes he would give us a ticket. It was like trying to find a parking space in London. Graham packed his bag and jumped ashore with the briefest farewells. Bridget and I pottered off downstream to find somewhere we could tie up in Austria. Surprisingly our imperious policeman didn't seem to mind that we were effectively leaving Germany for Austria along what the Bavarians call the 'sausage equator' without any paperwork or customs inspection at all.

The Accidental Sailor

For poor Graham driving the ailing Rover and the trailer back, things didn't go quite as smoothly with the border officials. He arrived back at Dover to be quizzed by the English customs officers.

So you took a boat down to the Danube on the trailer. Where is the boat now?
Graham explained that the boat and me and Bridget were somewhere in Austria and headed on down the Danube.
So when is it coming back?
It isn't. They are going to the Black Sea.
Hmm. If you would like to drive into the inspection shed sir.

Graham later told me how they examined all around the trailer and then started on the car. Everything came out and then they took all the lining out of the doors, the boot, dismantled the glove compartment, looked everywhere they thought Graham might have hidden whatever illegal goods he was trying to smuggle into England. They looked utterly baffled when they couldn't find anything and ultimately had to let Graham go.

4 Austria

Passau, Graham and the policeman receded into the misty distance as we were swept downriver looking for somewhere to tie up for the night. Fifteen kilometres from Passau I spied a small harbour at Obernzell with some little motorboats in it. The entrance was narrow and a bit tricky, but motoring up into the current we got in and didn't run aground. *Rozinante* was the biggest boat in the tiny harbour, a first for us. We ate a quiet meal on board and then got some sleep before the morrow. We were in Austria and this next section of the Danube winds between the high land on either side where the river has cut through the valley, a spectacular though mellow riverscape peppered with castles and Schloss and the holiday homes of the better off Austrian folk.

26th June We set off in the morning and settled down to enjoy the river and the sights on either side. By this time we were working well together, getting to know the boat and relaxing in the sun that had miraculously come out to bless this part of the Danube. The little boat was easy to nudge in and out of harbours, tie up in locks, to nose into tiny gaps. This just seemed too easy.

Just past Obermuhl there was a sudden clunk that sent a shudder through the boat and stopped the engine dead. I looked over the side to see a water-logged tree trunk drift lazily astern of *Rozinante*, a yellow gash on its top where the propeller had hit it. In Regensburg Joe from the motorboot club had told me to keep a good lookout for bits of lumber and tree trunks in the river. These bits of river flotsam were, he told me, the biggest danger to small boats on the river. He showed me a boat from the club with its propeller shattered after hitting a lump of wood.

All the way from Regensburg I had heeded Joe's advice and had carefully zigzagged around any bits of wood we spotted.

Large trees could usually be seen from the branches sticking up out of the water, but water-logged planks and old tree stumps or trunks were more difficult to spot. And this was one I had missed dammit. I re-started the engine, listened carefully to its tune as it beat away, climbed inside under the cockpit to check the propeller shaft, and with bated breath put the engine into and out of gear. Nothing appeared to have been damaged.

The Danube winds almost back on itself between the steep valley sides. We watched the castles and Schloss glide by and life seemed good. A little further on I spotted a small pleasure harbour at Untermuhl and nosed *Rozinante* into it. The village, really more of a hamlet, though the impressive stone houses belie the normal notions of a hamlet, is a perfect little place and what's more has a perfect little harbour. After a walk ashore and a quiet dinner on board I had forgotten about the incident. It would come back to haunt me and come close to putting an end to the whole voyage.

27th June The next day we set off again in sunshine. The Danube plunges steeply down the valley and so there are a number of weirs and locks along the way to stem the flow of the river. We use the same method in the locks that we used in *Roulette* in the French canals with just a single line from the foredeck to a bollard in the lock and back down to the cockpit. By adjusting the line we can keep *Rozinante* alongside the lock wall.

Linz sits on the right bank of the Danube and we tie up on the high-sided dock off the city. We haven't been here long before a man pops up to tell us we can't stay there, but if we carry on

II Rozinante

a bit there is a harbour where we will find a berth. Sure enough a bit further on a huge basin opens up with some pontoons for little boats on the north side. And it's not far from downtown Linz. We spend a few days enjoying the cafés and window shopping in this elegant and quite shi-shi Austrian city. Old fashioned trams trundle around the main streets making it easy to get places. The locals all seem an affluent lot, well dressed and prosperous. We try to spruce up on *Rozinante* before we go for a wander around town, but I fear we look tatty compared to the natty burghers, a little out of place drinking Vienna coffee and eating sacher-torte with undisguised pleasure.

29th June   Off again and everything is going well. The old Volvo Penta is beating away with its single lung and taking us gently along the Danube. We stop for the night in Grein. There are lots of little pleasure boat harbours or pontoons along the way and no-one seems to mind if we nose in and spend the night there.

This narrow section of the river means it can be a bit tricky when the barge trains come along. Commercial traffic on the Danube is a frightening experience for the first one or two encounters, after that we are a bit more relaxed about it. Traffic normally keeps to the starboard side of the river as is normal practice. However barge convoys, both pusher-tugs, but more particularly barge tows, often need to line themselves up for corners or difficult sections of the channel from the wrong side of the river. The tugs, both pusher-tugs and towing tugs, and powered barges, have a board signal showing you the side to pass on, but you will normally see the flashing strobe lights they are required to use showing the side to pass on, before you ever see the board signal. Commercial traffic has right of way on the river and any pleasure boat skipper who obstructs one of these river leviathans needs his head examined - you wouldn't step out in front of a double-decker bus so don't put a small pleasure craft in front of several thousand tons of a barge train and the thousands of horsepower pushing or pulling it.

30th June   Below Grein there are a series of rapids and standing waves that were previously feared on the Danube, though they have now been tamed by the new barrages built since the war. At least so I had read. The river is squeezed into a narrow section of twists and turns down the valley, creating standing waves and tricky currents.

The Schwalleck rapids were a doddle, but lining *Rozinante* up for the Strudel, such a sweet sounding name, I had to leave room for a pusher tug charging upstream. The wash from the tug and the standing waves of the Strudel pushed a wall of water over *Rozinante*. Water poured in around the front hatch drowning bags, books and food. It squeezed in through the hatch, through the windows and dolloped into the cockpit. Bridget and I clutching the coamings in the cockpit were soaked through.

There was no danger. It was the realisation that *Rozinante* was not as waterproof as we had thought which shocked us. If we were to take her across the Black Sea into Turkey she needed to be more watertight than this deluge had shown her to be. At the Hausstein rapids I concentrated on lining *Rozinante* up into the waves and disturbed water with great care, probably a bit exaggerated after our earlier deluge, and not a drop came on board. As it turned out the standing waves of the Strudel and the wash from the pusher tug provided the worst dousing *Rozinante* encountered on the whole trip. Perhaps old Father Danube had administered a friendly early warning to keep us on our toes.

II Rozinante

At Stein und Krems I spotted another little harbour and pottered in to find a berth. A friendly local boater pointed a berth out and helped us tie up. He seemed quite impressed we had come down from Regensburg.

Where are you going next?
Down the Danube to the Black Sea.
His face clouded over.
You are going down there? To the communist countries.
I nodded. He looked worried.
Listen. It is not like Austria and Germany down there. It is best to go back to Regensburg.
We nodded and, his job done, he wandered off shaking his head. The silly Englishers on board the small boat are still determined to carry on.

2nd July   We stayed a day and the following morning our friendly local returned and I asked where to berth in Vienna. He advised me that the best place to be was in the marina at Kahlenbergerdörf on the outskirts of Vienna. We motored off and eventually we found the entrance to the river at Kahlenbergerdörf. I turned into the river mouth and berthed at a pontoon. In the office I was greeted by Herr Klein.

Call me Mr Small. You are the small boat out there with the English flag. Now you want a berth, no?
Now there is a nice peaceful berth over there.
He pointed a spot out.
You are are going all the way down the Donau, no - we're used to a few boats going down, now not so many. Too many problems in Bulgaria and Romania. You know Romania.
I said I had been there on my earlier trip by land.
Then you know, the poorest country in Europe, really the

poorest, you will see poor people like never before.

Mr Small showed us where to climb under the fence to get in at night, where to catch the train into Vienna, where his office was in case we needed anything, then excused himself and trotted off to tell the crane operator something. Whenever I saw him Mr Small was perpetually out of breath running around the marina, talking breathlessly to everyone who came within earshot. Whenever we walked through the marina to or from the boat Mr Small would appear, call a greeting over his shoulder with a few words of advice, excuse himself and dash off on an urgent errand.

You have metal canisters for fuel, no, you need metal as it is against the law in those countries to put fuel in plastic cans.

One of the really valuable tips Mr Small gave us was to wander up the road where there were Heuriges. Heurige is green or young white wine made from local vineyards. The restaurants produced plates of sausages, roast pork and chicken, sauerkraut and salad on sunny verandahs looking over the Danube. And of course carafes of heurige. I could have stayed here for weeks. We shopped and shopped some more for provisions and anything we thought we might need once into the communist countries and also took in a few museums and art galleries in downtown Vienna. This was, we thought, to be our last taste of freedom and plenty before we burst through the Iron Curtain..

5th July Odile arrives to join us for three weeks. Somehow we cram three people into *Rozinante's* crowded bubble of interior space. Already I'm having doubts about the sanity of this arrangement. Odile is young and attractive, but a naif when it comes to travel and she knows nothing about boats. Bridget is a seasoned traveller and knows lots about boats and boat

II Rozinante

etiquette. I think this could all be a bit of a mistake. Of my own making.

8th July   We left Kahlenbergerdörf on a sunny noonday morning. Mr Small saw us off.

You have all the visas. Good. You have enough food for Bulgaria and Romania. Good. You be careful.

He was still calling advice after us as the Danube picked *Rozinante* up and rocketed us downstream. Around the docks at Vienna are cruise boats, barges, trip boats and tugs milling about in Vienna's backyard. A large number of barge trains and other boats still use Vienna proper, though the main commercial harbour is downstream of Vienna itself.

Several bridges connect the new suburbs on the east bank to old Vienna. The brown waters of the Danube, coloured by the mud and lime picked up from the bottom and discoloured by oil and diesel, are tunnelled through the narrow gap of the new channel past suburbs and commercial docks that hide old Vienna, old Hapsburg Vienna that is, from the river. Hainburg on the border between Austria and Czechoslovakia is nearly 50 kilometres from Vienna, but the current whirled us down to it in just three hours without the engine doing very much work at all. I had hoped to spend the night here before going on into Czechoslovakia, but there was nowhere to tie up except at the customs pontoon where we could not stay the night. Customs stamped our passports and with a quizzical look at the overloaded boat wished us what I took to be the Austrian equivalent of bon voyage.

5 Czechoslovakia

Before we got to Bratislava an open launch with several soldiers in it came out to motion us into a pontoon on the right bank. They had rifles slung over their shoulders, but the fresh faced boys in uniforms seemed more interested in sneaking sidelong glances at Bridget and Odile than in threatening any of us. I steered *Rozinante* into the pontoon and it was indicated that we should stay there until the relevant officials were summoned from Bratislava.

Three officials turned up after half an hour, khaki-green uniforms, a few brass stars, peaked caps. The youngest, a pallid young man with a thin moustache, took our passports and went into a little hut by the pontoon to do the paperwork. The other two, a good looking fair haired man in his thirties with a smooth manner I disliked, and a fatter one, breathless and looking a little ill at ease, came on board. They each managed to find somewhere to sit in *Rozinante's* cramped interior and looked around them. The smooth blond picked up a magazine Odile had brought with her, *Actuel*, and began thumbing through it. Suddenly he looked up and I noticed with horror that he had stopped at an article on Stalin in it, old black and white photographs of inmates in the Gulag, photographs of Stalin meeting world leaders, old posters in bright Soviet realism.

Do you have any literature on Czechoslovakia?
I showed him the few guidebooks on central Europe I had on board.
No ideology?
I shook my head wondering just what constituted ideology.

II Rozinante

He beckoned the fat man over to look at the pictures in the article on Stalin. They pointed to this and that in the photographs, in the way you look over holiday snaps, gesticulating and chattering to each other. One photograph showing labour camp inmates seemed to puzzle them, as if shedding new light on their lives, and they contemplated it silently, finally turning the page after frowning at each other.

The fat official looked up and remembered he was supposed to be doing a job. He made a half-hearted effort to search the boat, but the pile of baggage inside eventually defeated him and he sat down with a tired look on his face, He mimed taking a picture with a camera and I pulled out our impressive arsenal of cameras. He mimed a radio and I showed him the radio cassette player. He mimed a rifle and I smiled. No. He jotted down a few details on a scrap of paper and this seemed to exhaust his energy reserves. He resumed looking at the *Actuel* with the colleague who I had decided was the intelligence man.

By now they had moved on from the article on Stalin and were discussing the advertisements. Any menace they might have conveyed disappeared in their boyish pleasure at the lingerie advertisements. A cough outside announced that the harassed looking official who had been doing the papers was back. He handed our passports to us and indicated that we should follow the launch to the port in Bratislava.

The launch roared off down the river and though I put *Rozinante* on full ahead, it disappeared around a bend. A minute later it was back again as the officials realised they would have to idle downstream if they were going to escort us. The buildings of Bratislava appeared and we passed them towards the gantries that picked out the commercial port. The escort launch left us at the entrance and I rattled along inside the huge basin, happy to be out of the current, looking for a place to berth. At the end I saw a large steel yacht tied up with just enough space astern of it to get *Rozinante* into.

The yacht parked in front of us was a proper ocean-going beast. Apart from the dull grey it was painted, the yacht looked much like any fifteen metre ocean-going yacht you might run into anywhere in the world, a little too rugged and practical to be called a beauty, but beautiful to any cruising sailor's eye. I had heard of *Kondor* before, of the owner Zdenek Polasek, of his labour of love building this boat.

I met Zdenek when he returned late at night. I went on board and somehow, through my primitive German and sign language aided by squiggles and figures on a note pad, we understood each other. Zdenek was a miner, and *Kondor* represented his dream fuelled by years of hard work. He showed me a photograph of the launch of *Kondor*, the two masts stepped in schooner rig, sails bent on, bedecked with flags. As I looked over the boat finished in loving detail, I realised everything that could be was made from steel. Cleats, davits, hand-holds, the wind generator aft, stanchions, rails, the dorade boxes and cowls. Even the masts and booms were steel as Czechoslovakia does not produce the sort of aluminium extrusion used in mast construction. The engine was a marinised truck engine in an immaculate engine room. Anything Zdenek could not make or modify he imported at vast cost. To buy his autopilot Zdenek had to work for two years.

In the saloon of *Kondor* over a bottle of wine I asked him the inevitable question: when was he going to head down river to the sea? Zdenek's face hardened. He went over to a locker and pulled a pile of papers out and handed them to me. It took a while before I deciphered what he was saying. The authorities would not give him a visa to leave. He showed his repeated applications for a visa and then showed me some more papers. When I understood what he was saying I realised why he was close to tears. Five years before his son had attempted to escape across the border into Germany. He had been shot before he got across. Not only had Zdenek lost his son, he also lost the right to leave. The authorities had denied him permission to leave because his son had attempted to leave without it. Catch 22.

Why not just go?

He explained that while he wanted to sail to all the places in the world he had read about, to the Indian Ocean, the Pacific Islands, the Caribbean, the Mediterranean, he wanted to return to Czechoslovakia. It was his country. He did not want to be an exile from the country of his birth.

And what if they never give you permission? What will happen to *Kondor*?

Zdenek hoped that his beloved yacht would remain, a testament to the will of a man who hoped.

When I die, *Kondor* will remain.

I wonder what Zdenek is doing now. Sailing around the Mediterranean in my own yacht *Tetranora* after the Velvet Revolution, I kept looking in every harbour for a battleship-grey yacht flying the Czechoslovakian flag, but I didn't see Zdenek. Neither of us sitting in the saloon of *Kondor* that night could dream of what was to happen so dramatically with the Velvet Revolution, though I have the feeling Zdenek knew something would happen. When I asked if there was anything I could do for him, plead his case in London or write to the newspapers, he asked me to hold off for a bit, he would write to let me know if he thought that course of action was necessary. I remember being puzzled and asked Zdenek if something was in the air, did he have other options? He had smiled and indicated there was a possibility.

10th July What I hadn't done when we left Bratislava was to report to the patrol base before we left. I assumed that all we had to do was clear into the next port at Komarno and then clear out of Czechoslovakia. We had hardly gone any distance down river before I spotted a patrol boat speeding after us, so I slowed down to see what was up. The soldiers in the patrol boat motioned us to go back and I mimed that it was impossible. I turned *Rozinante* around into the current and gave it full throttle. While I could point up-stream, *Rozinante* was still going downstream, swept backwards by the strong current, the propeller churning the water. The current in the Danube below Bratislava has to be around seven knots. I motioned helplessly to the soldiers who looked on bewildered - they had orders to get me back, but it was evident that this was impossible.
While they radioed back to base I was swept gently backwards down river while motoring against it at full speed ahead. The officer in charge finally got permission to check our papers at a pontoon downstream and roared off ahead of us, indicating we should follow. A few kilometres later the patrol boat tied up at a pontoon and I turned *Rozinante* into the current and drifted somewhat violently backwards and alongside. The soldiers grabbed the ropes Bridget threw and we were tied up, though bucking about furiously in the current. It took a minute for the

officer to check our papers and with a smile or two from the soldiers we departed.

The patrol boats buzzed us repeatedly as we pottered down the river until I surmised that it was probably the scantily clad bodies of Bridget and Odile that interested the soldiers rather than our progress in Czechoslovakia. As Odile stepped below she suddenly turned and said, there's water in the cabin. I handed the helm to Bridget and jumped below. Water was slopping over the cabin sole. I pulled the engine cover off to discover the engine compartment was awash, the fly-wheel spraying water everywhere. Bridget stopped the engine and began pumping. I checked the obvious places first, the inlet for the cooling water, the inlet hose to the engine, the exhaust, the stern gland. Nothing.

Once most of the water had been pumped out I restarted the engine and edged over to the side of the river where we anchored in a metre of water. While Bridget and Odile pumped to keep the water level down I crawled into the bowels of the boat to find the problem. Around the stern tube, which houses the propeller shaft, water was gushing in at the outboard end. It was serious. The little bilge pump needed a hundred strokes every fifteen minutes and there was no way we could keep that up for long. *Rozinante* was sinking. I remembered the log we had hit with the propeller in Austria - it must have damaged the shaft which in turn damaged the stern tube.

Where were all the green patrol boats now I needed one? I reasoned that if I could communicate the problem to the officer on a patrol boat then he would tow *Rozinante* to Komarno which was about twelve kilometres downstream. There I would have to find a way to get the boat hauled out of the water and find someone or somewhere to make repairs. Although I had a back-up outboard engine for *Rozinante*, in the confusion of things to do before leaving I hadn't checked to see if it fitted the outboard bracket on the back. When I tried it the bracket crumbled, its wooden pad rotted from the inside out. Bridget had a few things to say about the preparation for the trip, though thankfully she saved them for later.

Eventually a patrol boat came around the bend in the river and I waved frantically for them to come over. After a lot of bumping and bashing the patrol boat was tied alongside and I began a mime show. The boat is sinking. I pumped, drew a picture of *Rozinante* going down, drew a crane hauling the boat out of the water, pointed to Komarno and indicated that we needed a tow to get there. The officer finally understood our problem and radioed to his base. His superior refused permission for the patrol boat to tow us to Komarno. All the officer could do was tow us to the river bank.

He was obviously upset about his superior's decision and radioed again. A voluble conversation ensued, though the outcome was the same, he was only able to tow us to the bank. The officer raised his two hands palm uppermost in the universal gesture of despair and helplessness; the soldiers nodded in sympathy. I motioned that I would get to Komarno somehow, made a gesture towards the patrol boat's radio that was greeted by sly smiles, and thanked them for their help. There was no way I was going to maroon *Rozinante* in a swamp in Czechoslovakia.

After the patrol boat had departed I started the engine, hauled up the anchor and we drifted downstream. I left the engine in neutral and only put it into gear to line *Rozinante* up for bridges

II Rozinante

or to avoid a barge train. The current whooshed us down at around six knots and it wasn't long before Komarno came into view. Cranes and gantries gave me some hope that I could find a way to get *Rozinante* hauled out. I swung into the commercial basin and there at the entrance was the patrol boat base complete with a crane for hauling the patrol boats out. It was perfect.

I swung around to approach the base and heard a whistle. The guard on duty was waving me away. I came a little closer and tried pointing to the crane and then to *Rozinante*. I pointed to Odile pumping away on the bilge pump. He waved us away pointing back into the Danube and shouting, Kontrol! Kontrol! I needed to do something soon so I pointed to my shoulder, and then ashore, in a gesture I hoped would indicate that I wanted to see a superior officer. The guard pointed to his shoulder, unslung the automatic rifle on his back and, though he did not point it at us, motioned us away from the base in in a manner that clearly meant, 'You do not come any closer'. I motored over to where some barges were berthed on the opposite side of the basin, found a space and tied up.

While Bridget and Odile pumped, I went ashore to somehow find help. Halfway along the quay I met a group of seamen on their way back from a run ashore, most of them much the worse for wear after a day on the town. They bantered drunkenly with me while I attempted to find one who spoke English. None did, though luckily the only sober one spoke some German.

Namen Karol - Charlie, Charlie.

I grabbed his arm and dragged him back to *Rozinante* where in a flash he understood my mime, the girls pumping and the need to haul the boat out. We tried the dock cranes first and although an operator was willing to do the job, there was nowhere to put *Rozinante* out of the way of the railway wagons being shunted around on either side of the cranes. We went back to Charlie's boat, a huge pusher tug, where he was first mate. Telephone calls were made, but with no effect. In the end I went back to *Rozinante*, weary and despondent. Odile, not used to hard physical work, could pump no longer. Her hands were cramped together from holding the bilge pump handle. Bridget was tiring.

In the basin I had noticed a patch of muddy bank that sloped gradually upwards, next to a huge shipyard that built and repaired barges. I decided to run *Rozinante* aground, stern first, in the hope of getting the stern tube into shallower water when there would be less pressure forcing water inside. And at least *Rozinante* would not sink even if she half-filled with water. I explained all this to Charlie and motored over to the bank.

Going full astern I drove *Rozinante* up as far as I could, then took a line ashore and using a crude purchase on a pulley block, with the girls heaving waist deep in the water, we got the boat up as far as we could. It seemed to work, there was less water coming in, but still more than enough to require pumping every fifteen minutes. Charlie appeared an hour later, a smile on his face.

Morgen, Morgen? Raymond, Raymond.
He held up six fingers.
Morgen, morgen.

He pointed at the barge slipway. If I understood Charlie correctly we were going to be hauled out in the shipyard in the morning, at six o'clock. I tried to find out what had happened, who Charlie had contacted, but my German was not up to it. I sat up the rest of the night and pumped.

11th July   Sometime in the early morning I must have dropped off because Odile woke me to say the boat was filling up with water and her socks were getting wet. I pumped for half an hour with a cup of coffee and watched the dawn come up. At five-thirty workmen began appearing. There were six of them. One of the slipway cradles was lowered and I was motioned to motor *Rozinante* out and back onto it. Bridget and Odile were desperately hauling clothes on. By the time they were up the boat was out of the water and workmen were examining the propeller and shaft fitting, two of them crawled into the engine compartment and began dismantling the coupling. Like magic in the early morning sun *Rozinante* was being taken apart for repairs.

Bridget and Odile were taken away by a man who appeared to be in charge, to a restaurant, where they changed money and sat down to breakfast. I stayed to see if I could be of any help to the trio who were doing the work, the Master, the Bulgar and the Pharaoh. I never learnt the real names of any of them, though I asked several times. As work progressed it became apparent that more work was needed to put *Rozinante* right than had first been thought. It was impossible to buy spares for the engine in Czechoslovakia and so the Bulgar and Pharaoh took a pattern off the old stern tube and constructed a new one.

The propeller shaft was removed and checked to see if it was straight by a young blond woman who looked like she had just popped out of a magazine from some article on life in communist Czechoslovakia. She knew her craft and operated the lathe like a pro. A new stern tube was made up and threaded on to the old fitting. The stern gland was fibre-glassed into place.

With all this work going on I was worried about the cost of it all. I asked the Bulgar, who had a smattering of English, how much this was all going to cost. The only reply I got was, this is a socialist state - you are our guest - this is a socialist state. What the hell, I thought, if a bill is presented later that I can't pay, at least *Rozinante* will be afloat rather than at the bottom of the river.

Things got more mysterious in the afternoon as the trio toiled on, obviously unhappy at the extent of the work. The Bulgar nodded at me.

We have been told to stay until the work is finished. I have to stay here.
I asked who had told him to stay, curious about who had ordered the work.
My boss, the chief. But he has been told to help you.
Who told him?
The Bulgar didn't reply and carried on with his work.

In the afternoon two soldiers arrived to ask what was going on. They asked for our passports, the boat papers, then started to interrogate the Bulgar and the Pharaoh. The exchange was heated. Then the Master appeared and with two sharp words shut the soldiers up. I don't know what he said, but it cowed the soldiers who quickly left. The Bulgar made an abrupt arm gesture towards the departing soldiers.

They are a big shit for us, they don't work, they have money, I spit on them.

II Rozinante

The work was nearing the end and I thought it time to break out the whisky.

By early evening the work was finished. No one appeared to demand payment and the Bulgar was still keeping to his lines when I enquired how much it was going to cost.
We are a socialist state.

Over whisky I gave the trio twenty dollars each which I knew was worth more than a week's wages at black market rates. By late evening *Rozinante* was lowered back into the water and though the repairs would not hold up to any excessive hard motoring, they would have to do for now. I mean *Rozinante* wasn't sinking any more, Odile wasn't getting her feet wet and Bridget's hands had recovered from the pumping. Things felt cheery.

The Bulgar advised me to get proper replacements for the bits they had fabricated as soon as I could. As it turned out the repairs had to last until *Rozinante* got to Turkey some 1700 nautical miles later.

12th July   To the Zavody Tazkeho Strojarstva shipyard in Komarno and to the Master, Pharaoh and to the Bulgar and the beautiful blond lathe operator, I extend my grateful thanks. I still don't know who ordered the work to be done, or why, though I have one or two theories. In the morning we motored over to Charlie's pusher tug and tied alongside. Charlie introduced us to the captain, who spoke some English and we sat down to breakfast. Over thick black coffee I asked the captain whether payment was required. He smiled.

You are a small boat in trouble on the river. Czechoslovakia had to help you.
But who ordered the work?

He didn't know. I pulled out my last bottle of whisky and handed it to Charlie.
For your help.
He refused to take it. I insisted, but Charlie was having none of it. Then I had a brain wave.

For the boat. For your boat, for everyone on the boat.

Charlie accepted it on behalf of the boat.

I wonder what labyrinthine events the repairs to *Rozinante* set in motion. Someone high up in the command chain probably ordered the work carried out to get rid of the troublesome English boat. Otherwise we might have been stuck in Czechoslovakia for ages. I hope that there were no recriminations to anyone involved. I felt as if I was defecting from some responsibility I should have sorted out before leaving Czechoslovakia. I also kept looking over my shoulder to see if a patrol boat would speed out to apprehend us before we got to the Hungarian customs post on the other side of the Danube. None did.

6 Hungary

13th July   Clearing into Hungary was easy and relaxed. Since launching in Regensburg *Rozinante's* mast had been down, tied onto the pulpit and the cabin top. In Esztergöm we put the mast up for the first time on the river. It was a pretty small mast, less than the length of the boat, even for an alleged 18 footer, so it didn't increase our air height hugely. Two of us had it up in no time. The rigging is rudimentary, just a forestay and cap shrouds. No cross-trees, backstay, or much else. The bright reddy orange plastic sails are out, the mainsail stowed on the boom and the jib hanked on the forestay ready to go. *Rozinante* is ready to go sailing for the first time, well my first time.

The repairs to the stern tube mean we can use the diesel sporadically, but from here we will sail whenever we can. *Rozinante's* mast is so short, about 23ft above water level, we will fit under all the bridges with the exception of the lowest bridge at Novisad in Yugoslavia.

When we arrived at Esztergöm we were greeted at the pontoon by a wiry gentleman who seemed like something out of one of the old aristocratic Hungarian estates. He bowed stiffly from the waist.

My name is Stefan - welcome to Esztergöm.

He had an old world charm and a dignity that contrasted vividly with anything I had encountered in Czechoslovakia. He was more Hapsburg than anyone in Vienna. He directed us to a fish restaurant up the arm of the Danube where a fish meal was served up that was absolutely superb. Hungary is like this, full of pleasant surprises that, even before the 'Iron Curtain' fell, turned stereotypes of Eastern Bloc countries around and forced you to look at the country and its people with unblinkered eyes.

14th July   Budapest is not far from Esztergom. We arrived in Budapest after sailing most of the way from Esztergöm. The wind tends to blow up or down a river, more or less, so we will either be running with the wind or beating into it. The river widens here where the great Magyar Plain starts to open out and there is more room on the river to avoid barge trains and other traffic in a small sailing boat bobbing along and trying to sail. It's the current which is doing the lion's share of the work with the sails giving us a bit of direction.

Sailing with a current running is odd. You can put the helm over and little happens if you don't have enough speed through the water. You don't really notice this that much because the current is zooming you along anyway and everything has the appearance of a boat in motion with sails up. It's just that often the sails aren't doing that much except looking pretty in a reddy orange plastic sort of way in *Rozinante's* case. I put *Rozinante* into a small commercial canal at the upriver end of Budapest for the night and tie alongside the quay.

15th July   We move from the commercial quay to a pontoon for a rowing club at Margaret Island near the centre of Budapest. The caretaker seems a little inebriated, but friendly for all that. Too friendly as it turns out.

Budapest is like a poor cousin to Vienna. The grand Baroque buildings are there, even the wonderful coffee and cake shops, the churches and little follies of the Hapsburg, but without the spit and polish of Vienna. Somehow it is all the more approachable for that and we spend one of those relaxed and easy days exploring the heart of the city, split by the Danube.

II *Rozinante*

After exploring Budapest we return to Rozinante where the caretaker starts to plead with me.

Give me one of your women.

I attempt to explain that they are not 'my women', and that neither of them feels like spending the night with an inebriated caretaker. I spend the night sleeping in the cockpit with a hammer beside me while the caretaker stalked the pontoon with a bottle of local fire-water and a mournful look on his face.

16th July I'm pretty relieved when morning comes as I must have dozed off for a while from my guard duties. We move to another basin further downstream where we tie up to the pontoon of another rowing club. It is miles from the centre of Budapest, but there are buses and cheap taxis and no weird grovelling caretaker.

This is the only city in the world where I have hailed a taxi and asked him to take me to a nice restaurant for dinner. We all pile into the little Trabant, the two stroke people's car made in East Germany, and career off leaving clouds of two stroke smoke behind us. The taxis are so cheap here, and sterling so strong against the Hungarian forint, that I feel no fiscal fear doing this. We eat a long drawn out feast on the outskirts of Budapest complete with a gypsy band that has that eerie instrument, the zither, in its line-up. The food is all reminiscent of Vienna or the Hapsburg - I have a wonderful trout in a cream sauce with flaked almonds on top – quite rich but well executed. We trundle back to the boat in the Trabant, replete and ready for the Danube.

17th July   When we leave in the morning we are escorted out by 40 or so kayaks from the club, all waving and careering about and paddling furiously to keep up with us. We anchor for the night in a huge basin at Dunanjvaros, swim, and have a leisurely dinner in the cockpit. There is a heat wave killing hundreds in Greece and Turkey and though temperatures here are not up to those in the Mediterranean, it is very hot and sticky. It feels like summer on the river.

18th July   Things are getting a bit tense on board between Bridget and Odile. Bridget gets frustrated at Odile's skills, or lack of them, on board and complains that she hasn't cooked once on board.
It's not a cruise boat. You should help more.

I attempt to mediate between Bridget's brusque nature and acerbic comments and Odile's ennui.

Time for a halt and fortuitously a pontoon appears off a camping ground. We tie up and I discover there are little cabins to rent. I book one and we retire for a bit of life ashore away from the confines of the small boat. I trail a line off the back of the boat and we take turns jumping in and being swept rapidly downstream until we can grasp the line and haul ourselves back on board. The tension evaporates in silly water games in the hot sunshine.

At least it does until a police car pulls up and we are ordered out of the water. Here we go, I thought, the paperwork trail begins. They request our passports, boat papers and quiz us on what we are doing here in Hungary. It turns out they are not that interested in the paperwork, but for our safety swimming in the swift currents of the Danube. It is prohibited and so I assure them we will not do it again and off they go.

II Rozinante

When I go to the camping ground office to register things are not so straightforward and the manager says he must keep the passports and send them to the authorities in Paks downriver. Visitors to Hungary are automatically registered with the police at hotels and camping grounds and so our passports were impounded because we had been in Hungary for six days and had not registered. So tomorrow we need to stop in Paks to sort things out.

19th July   Paks is not far away and I find somewhere to tie up and then trot off to find the police. This takes a bit of doing, but eventually I find the right office and I'm requested to sit down and wait. Uniformed officers take a few details, bizarrely asking for passports, and then I am shown into another office where I am grilled by a plain clothes man, politely but firmly, who eventually hands our precious passports back after noting down my story.

20th July   Baja. Odile leaves on the train for Paris so it is just Bridget and me on board now. In every way that is a bit of a relief as Odile knows little about travelling abroad, let alone behind the Iron Curtain. Bridget, who had been threatening to leave, seems a lot more relaxed.

In Baja my mission is to hunt out someone to make up a new outboard bracket. The stern tube repairs in Czechoslovakia are holding up, but will not last for long, so I intend to sail and use the outboard, keeping the diesel in reserve for emergencies and for any difficult manoeuvring we have to do. I wander around Baja asking people and eventually I'm directed to a café to ask Andrei where to repair the bracket.

Andrei speaks a bit of English and when he understands what I want motions me to his car and we whirl off down the streets. We pull up at a field and I see the ferro-cement hull of a yacht. Andrei gets a ladder out and we climb up on board. A bit like *Kondor* in Bratislava, many of the fittings have been fabricated from steel. The 35 foot boat doesn't have a mast and rigging yet, but Andrei assures me it will be ready soon – made from steel. Inside it is all finished and varnished.

One more year. Then I leave. Then I leave for the Mediterranean.
Are there others building boats in Hungary?
Sure. Sure.

Somehow I hadn't thought of a nascent yachting population on the Danube, but then escaping from a Czechoslovakia or a Hungary has a bit more grunt to it than the easy voyages we make from the West. Easy in that no-one stops us going. Easy in that there is a whole yachting community, chandlers, magazines.

Andrei takes me to a carpenters shop where a new bit of hardwood is soon cut and bolted to the bracket. When we get back to *Rozinante* I have a bit of a rummage inside and find a couple of yachting magazines. Andrei's face lights up and he almost sheds a tear as he thumbs through them.

Thank you. Thank you so much.

Such a little gift for so much pleasure from the recipient.

24th July   We motor down to Mohacs to clear out. The outboard moves *Rozinante* along at around 2½-3 knots which with 3 knots or so of current is enough to keep us going at a respectable pace. We have to clear out of Hungary here so I go up to the customs office. The officer there is a friendly soul who notes down the particulars, then goes back into his office to emerge grasping a telex covering an A4 page. He points to a name: Bertolotti, Odile Marie Susanne.

Where is she?

I realise the telex probably details everything known to the Hungarians about us from my interview in Paks with the plain clothes man featuring prominently. I explain that she has left by train for Paris several days ago.

No problems.

The amiable customs officer nods, and then takes the telex back to his office. The rest of the paperwork for clearing out is finished quickly - it was only the whereabouts of the third crew member which was worrying him.

7 Yugoslavia

25th July   We leave Mohacs and anchor for the night in the waterland just inside the Yugoslavian border. Just as Bridget serves the evening meal I notice the sky has changed colour to a greasy grey-black and that lightning is flickering around the horizon. I've read about these storms blowing off the Puzsta. Then I notice a line of white water advancing across the river. The storm hits us before we can get the anchor up properly, the wind blowing *Rozinante* over with waves drenching the boat in spray. The fury and suddenness of it is frightening, all the more so because it is so unexpected on a river.

We manage to get the anchor up and in a dusk punctuated by flashes of lightning and to the sound of the wind and waves fly downstream looking for somewhere to shelter. About ten kilometres down river I find a spot tucked in behind an island where we are safe from the waves, now 1-2 metres high and confused, with the wind against the current, kicked up by the storm off the Puszta.

Dinner is cold, but welcome after our little panic and the dash downriver. In the morning all is bright and calm, or relatively so with just a light breeze blowing downriver. The Danube spreads out into a wide waterland dotted with little islands and sandbars. The humid climate encourages thick almost jungle-like growth which coupled with the white sandy beaches of the islands and shore, gives the appearance of the tropics trapped in the middle of Europe. Bird and fish life is prolific, with white egrets, cormorants, herons, hoopoes, storks and birds of prey like the osprey everywhere. The Yugoslavs come here to camp on the islands and fish in the channels. Pottering through here it was possible to get lost if the channel markers weren't closely

II Rozinante

followed. Finding a place to stop for the night was easy, just choose an island and anchor in its lee.

This stretch of river is so unexpected and so at odds with what you might imagine the Danube is like that it mesmerises. It mesmerised us as we sailed gently down and I wasn't really concentrating too much when I spied a lot of aluminium dories and what looked like a floating pontoon bridge in front of us. It is a floating bridge. The army was evidently on exercises and I eyed the bridge, looking for a gap, as the current swept us down on it at a rate. Eventually a red flag went up and one of the dories pulled one of the pontoon sections open to let us through. Somehow I steered *Rozinante* through the gap to lots of waving and cheers from the soldiers.

26th July   We arrived at Vukovar in the late afternoon. There is a small harbour where I nose *Rozinante* into the bank. As we are tying up a dark haired man on a racing bike rides up to help.

You don't remember me. You asked me where to get petrol yesterday - on the river.

Now I remember him, idling down the river in a dinghy with a 4HP Tomos outboard, and as we were running low on petrol I had asked him where we could get some. I asked Mladen what had happened to him in the storm.

We simply keep goings. We are used to thems.

He went on to tell me how with several friends he had taken his 10 foot dinghy up to the Iron Gates dam for a holiday.

In Vukovar you are not a man without a boat.

I remembered that I had read about this section of the Danube being colonised by Germans who gained a reputation as first class seamen, much in demand on sea-going ships as well as river craft. I asked him if he had a German connection and learnt his grandparents had been German. His grandmother's maiden name was Braun and his grandfather Haufen. It is surprising this far down the river that there is such a strong and comparatively recent German connection. Not surprisingly the language of the river, right through to Romania, is German. There is another violent storm in the night though *Rozinante* is safe this time tucked up in the harbour.

We ate in a bar that night talking to the locals.

This one is Serb, I am Croat, he is Turkish but he is OK, that one Bulgaria.

In this beautiful old Baroque city, a bit down at heel, but alive and buzzing for all that, the different nationalities that inhabit Vukovar sit drinking and joking together. There is nothing in the air, no indication that in the summer of 1991 brother will kill brother, cousin will be set against cousin, that this happy band of drinkers will be fighting the ugly and brutal Battle of Vukovar. The atrocities are difficult to comprehend and include the massacre of patients from the hospital. It was a bloody and prolonged affair that levelled the wonderful old Baroque city. Journalists who said, in hindsight, that they could see what was going to happen in Vukovar were just using hindsight to somehow legitimise their lack of knowledge of the people and the feeling of place.

27th July   We left for Novisad in the morning with our precious petrol supplies renewed. Just before the town proper there is a

Watersport Club with a pontoon and a cheerful caretaker with a single toothed smile helps us tie up. I ask him if there is a Volvo Penta agent in the town, but there is no comprehension there. However he leads us over to a smooth-looking man sitting by an expensive motorboat who speaks English. When he understands I have a mechanical problem he motions me into the boat and in an instant we are off at 20 knots down the river to a mechanic he knows. I ask what he does, intrigued to discover how he owns an expensive Italian motorboat in socialist Yugoslavia.

I own a hotel. We are allowed private enterprise here you know. I do know, I just didn't think private ownership ran to hotels.

After racing up and down the river a few times it turns out there is no Volvo Penta agent in Novisad, but there is one in Belgrade.

28th July   At the pontoon I take down *Rozinante's* mast so we can pass under the lowest bridge on the Danube since Passau. The bridge at Novisad is a constant problem for barges and cruise boats which either have to dismantle the uppermost bridge deck or on the more modern craft have a hydraulic system to raise and lower the whole bridge deck. On *Rozinante* it's just a matter of undoing a few turn-buckles and then Bridget and I can just lower it and lash it to the pushpit.

It's a fair old hike to Belgrade, but there is still a good current swooshing us along. Finding somewhere to berth in Belgrade is difficult. I pottered down the River Sava to the quay where the trip boats and cruise boats berth, but was waved abruptly away. At the junction of the Danube and the Sava I tried mooring next to some dilapidated hulks which served as a boat club bar and restaurant, but was told to move on. Eventually I found an old commercial basin on the Danube where the amiable club members said I was welcome to stay. The surroundings, a collection of dilapidated buildings, a gravel works and some poisonous looking effluent leaking into the mud, were not the most salubrious, but at least it was safe and close to the centre of Belgrade.

29th July   In Belgrade I manage to track down the Volvo Penta agent, but he stocks few parts and doesn't have the stern tube fitting I need for the propeller shaft. Belgrade is one of my least favourite cities and this visit does nothing to make me like it any more than on previous visits. We decide we will leave tomorrow.

30th July   The outskirts of Belgrade are all apartment blocks in some sort of Socialist realist style, dull apartment blocks in a uniform dusty brown colour. Then comes the industrial areas with chimneys spouting dense clouds of smoke and spewing dirty brown effluent into the Danube. Once past this it all comes as a bit of a surprise to find islands covered in dense stands of trees and the banks of the river cut by fields of wheat and other arable crops. It's almost bucolic.

The Danube is slowed down now by the giant dam at the Iron Gates and so there is little current further downstream, perhaps a knot at most, helping us on our way. We potter along under sail until I spy a cut at Kostolac with some rickety catwalks out from the bank. We tie up alongside one and contemplate the flooded valley we will soon be entering.

31st July   A good breeze blowing down the river has meant we have sailed all day at speed, well at least the sort of speed you can get out of a Mirror Offshore 18. We stop in Veliko Gradiste for the night. The Danube is now over a kilometre wide in places, more like a lake than a river, though it is narrowing all the time as we get closer to the Iron Gates gorge. The people on the river have been unfailingly friendly. The fishermen hunched over their rods on the banks wave, the pusher-tug skippers honk their horns, pleasure boat owners scrutinise *Rozinante* with binoculars and then wave wildly, in the harbours the locals want to know where we have come from and where we are going. Moreover they know the river, about the places along the Danube, of the waterland before the Hungarian border teeming with fish and bird life, of the Gorge of Kazan and the Iron Gates dam, about the towns and villages along the way, of where the best slivovitza, the local plum brandy, comes from and where the best fish restaurants are. It's like they have a love affair with this river, something I can empathise with.

With the wind still howling down the river we decide to stay safely tied up for the day and see what the weather brings tomorrow.

2nd August   With a strong down-river wind *Rozinante* is creaming along. When the Iron Gates dam was completed and the valley flooded, islands in the river were covered by water. But at low water the dead branches of the trees on the islands stick up out of the water, a ghostly forest of dead branches, and on the section before Golubac we get lost in this dead forest, unsure of where the channel lies and spend an anxious hour threading our way out until we find the main channel again. The consequences of hitting a solid branch and ripping a hole in the bottom of *Rozinante* doesn't bear thinking about and for the first time I have a few qualms over the fact that we don't have a liferaft and not even much of a dinghy. The dinghy is a small inflatable not much bigger than a kid's beach toy.

That night we anchor at km 1013 behind a small promontory, tied to the branches of a dead tree for added security. It is a lonely place where every sound reverberates off the cliffs and where there seems to be not a soul about. This section of the river is like a huge lake surrounded by high hills and cliffs, a piece of Switzerland transported to Yugoslavia. When the Iron Gates lock gates were closed the water rose in the gorge submerging islands, towns, villages, farms, old forts and castles, forests and fields. Most of the old perils of the Danube were also submerged and now there are virtually no dangers to navigation in the buoyed channel. Except for those damned trees poking out of the water.

3rd August   The wind is up again and with a reefed main we are flying down river. I had read about the winds and storms of this region, but certainly didn't expect to encounter more than one. We do dally at Trajan's Tablet which commemorates his feat of building a road around the cliffs. It starts with the usual declaration of the positions he has held in the senate and how as Emperor he 'overcame the hazards of the mountains and the river - and opened this road'. The road, now flooded, was built by drilling holes in the cliff-face and supporting the road on poles sticking out from the cliffs. It was roofed over to stop attacks from the top of the cliffs and enabled Trajan and later emperors to conquer the wild region of Transylvania on the other side of the river. The tablet is set in the cliffs in a small inlet and once we poke our nose out we are whipped away downstream by the wind again.

II Rozinante

At the Iron Gates dam and lock at km 864 we wait to lock through. The wind is howling down the river and apparently the lock gates cannot be worked when the wind is up.

4th August   The wind is again too strong for the lock gates to be operated so we anchor off and spend an uncomfortable night being buffeted by the waves, up to 2 metres high, kicked up by the wind. Behind us the huge weir has water cascading down the outside and while it has a safety barrier around it, the thought of being washed down and over should the anchor drag keeps me awake most of the night.

5th August   At around lunchtime the gates open so we rush to get the anchor up and race over to the locks. I squeeze into a space at the back of the lock behind a cruise boat, two tugs and a barge and a steel Yugoslavian yacht which had been waiting with us. Once out of the lock we get side-swiped by the current from the weir and only just manage to get across to Prahovo, to the Yugoslavian customs post, to clear out of Yugoslavia before crossing into Bulgaria.

The old industrial harbour where I moored *Rozinante* at Prahovo is a grimy silted up place, surrounded by cranes and with fume-laden air that hurts your lungs when you breathe it in. I needed petrol and diesel before going into Bulgaria so I wandered ashore with the jerry-cans to fill up. The guard on the harbour gate asks what I want and when I tell him that it was *benzin* I needed, he pointed to the train tracks and said 'Negotin', holding up eight fingers to presumably show it was eight kilometres away. I started towards the railway tracks to be brought up by a shout of 'nein, nein', whereupon he mimed driving a car and pointed to one of the ramshackle houses shouting 'auto, auto - Ringo'. My German is pretty limited, non-existent really, and I was getting a little irked at being identified as a German with a very limited vocabulary - the German idiot on the river. I went up to the house and was greeted by a dark giant in greasy overalls who pointed at himself and said with a satisfied nod that he was Ringo. I pointed to the jerry-cans.

Ya, benzin, nix problem – Negotin.
He points to his battered Polski Fiat 650 in the garden.

100Km to 5 litres.

He is obviously proud of his little car. It didn't look capable of taking Ringo let alone me and two jerry cans as well. We had to push-start it and then jump in while it was still going, something about the clutch or lack of it Ringo had me understand, before we rattled off towards Negotin. Ringo had worked in Austria and so our conversation was in a bastard German and the English he had picked up from watching sub-titled films on television. He was married to a Romanian woman and had two children on the other side of the river in Romania. He was saving up to pay for them to come over to Yugoslavia, or rather paying for them to get passports to be able to leave.

Romania difficult, very difficult. Austria super, extra-prima, Yugoslavia not bad.

As we drove over the rough country roads parts kept dropping off the car and Ringo would stop and pick them up. First an exhaust bracket, then the next exhaust bracket, then the exhaust and silencer, then an unidentified bit and a couple of bolts. By the time we got to Negotin the Fiat sounded like a Sherman tank.

II Rozinante

I got my petrol and diesel, spent the rest of the dinar I had on bread, wine, biscuits, fruit juice, salami, anything I could find. Yugoslavia has an alarming rate of inflation and in a year's time my dinar would be worthless. We rattled back to Prahovo and caroomed down to the harbour where I paid Ringo the ten dollars we had agreed on in hard currency. It was a good deal for him, and in any case he was going to spend it on a good cause bribing a Romanian official to speed up his wife and children's passports.

8 Bulgaria

7th August   The border between Bulgaria and Yugoslavia has a fence right to the water's edge and ploughed earth on either side. A Bulgarian fishing boat, poaching on the Yugoslavian side of the river dispelled some of my fears about our reception in Bulgaria. On the bank watchtowers with radar on top and the occasional glint of light on binocular lenses tell us we are being watched and our progress monitored.

Before arriving in Bulgaria in *Rozinante* I had read in a recent book on the Danube that two yachts arriving in Bulgaria had to pay for two weeks stay in a Bulgarian hotel and that a German yacht had to return to Germany because of this fee. With this warning rolling around my head I arrived in Vidin wondering if a large sum of money, which in any case I didn't have, was going to be demanded of me. Just past the Timok River I was waved over to a Bulgarian gunboat moored by the bank and there, after checking our papers, I was told to clear in at Vidin. I berthed behind the ferry berth and went to find the relevant office.

In a dusty old office I found the harbourmaster, a grey-haired plump gentleman who seemed distressed at my presence. In pidgin German I understood that I was supposed to clear in at the port some two kilometres upstream. I got him to understand that it would take me a good hour to get upstream (the current in the Danube is still running at 3-4 knots off Vidin) and wheezing and sighing in sympathy, we went back to his office to ring the officials at the ferry port. Ten minutes later they were in the harbourmaster's office, smiles all round, a cursory check of the contents of *Rozinante*, and I was issued with papers to cruise the Danube in Bulgaria. No two weeks' hotel costs. A good deal less paper-work than in neighbouring Yugoslavia. And a politeness that made me feel welcome in Bulgaria, a welcome that remained wherever we went.

Vidin was once described as a fairy-tale city with spires and cupolas and minarets, but is now dominated by concrete high-rise buildings that obscure the old town and the fortress. When the Danube is in flood, it is almost an island, for behind the town, to the west, stretches a series of marshes which can attain a breadth of several miles. The watery defences of the town were unique for, apart from their natural strength, the moats which surrounded the old town could be filled at short notice with water from the Danube or its tributary the Topolovitza.

Although the modern town has obliterated much of the old, Vidin is still an interesting place to wander around with a market in the north and the bizarre bar-discos that the young Bulgarians frequent in droves to the east. You can still get the renowned spicy sausages of the area whose contents are probably best kept a secret, but are still good.

While Vidin in particular and Bulgaria in general does not have a great choice in its restaurants - the dishes on a menu do not guarantee they will be there that particular day - what you get is invariably tasty and the red wines of Bulgaria are always good, and often very good. You can't really say the same of the music and in one restaurant that had a live band playing, one of the locals sidled up to tell me they were going to play a special song for me. It took me until halfway through the song to recognise it was Elvis Presley's *Wooden Heart*, the rendition of it was so bad. Still the friendliness of the locals was 100%.

11th August   Just past Svistov an old arm of the Danube leads off behind a large wooded island. With Bridget calling the depths I take *Rozinante* down it to the village of Vardim. A police boat roars up and asks where we are going and appears unconcerned when I motion towards Vardim before they roar off upriver towards Svistov. The banks of the river and the island are thickly forested, the old channel is like some tropical creek except for the earth coloured houses of Vardim at the top of the curve of the channel. In Vardim there is virtually nothing to buy in the solitary shop and the beer in the one bar tastes like dishwater.

12th August   We arrive at Lom low on petrol again. Under the hot Balkan sun I have to walk 5 kilometres to the petrol station which was always 'just around the corner' when I ask the locals. On my quest for fuel I can't help noticing the incredible industry the locals here put into what can only be called mini-farms. Bulgarians are allowed to have their own private plots to grow vegetables and keep livestock. Every house has a patch of land so intensely cultivated that the green of growing vegetables, dotted with the red of tomatoes and peppers, is almost fluorescent. Many also have a small haystack for the livestock fitted into the scheme of things - mini farms lined up next to each other and seemingly all competing for who can grow more on less. It appears to be just the opposite of what I have heard about communal farms and state industry.

In these lower reaches the river spreads out into marshy lagoons on the Romanian side and cuts into the white limestone of the Balkans on the Bulgarian side. Islands are dotted about the river with glaring white sandy beaches and thick green vegetation behind, like a vision of the Amazon, a quite incongruous and unimagined geography for Europe.

This can get a bit tricky when navigating this stretch of river. The channel winds in and out of the islands and sandbanks and changes as parts of the river silt up. With scanty buoyage in places I often found I was navigating over the tops of submerged trees and bushes where I thought the channel should be according to charts of the river only five years old. Usually I retraced our course and waited until a barge tow came along so I could follow them along the main channel. In other places I took *Rozinante* up old channels and creeks to find quite idyllic spots where I could run the boat into the bank and we could spend the night in wonderful solitude or in a small village. The police never seemed to mind despite all the warnings about Bulgaria and its officials that I had encountered before leaving.

While the Romanian side is virtually deserted, the Bulgarians use the river for recreation in their droves. In places the Bulgarian beaches look like something from the crowded shores of the south of France with bodies everywhere, in the water, lying in the sun on bright beach towels under gaudy sun umbrellas, pottering about in canoes and kayaks and occasionally small runabouts.

14th August   At km 547 I nosed *Rozinante* up into an old arm of the Danube to moor off a small village for the night. We went ashore to find the usual gaggle of houses backed onto private gardens and livestock with horses and carts much in evidence carrying things about. In the small shop we found hardly anything to buy, some bread, cheese and some lolly-water in coca cola bottles that tasted of little else except sugar. Most of the vegetables in these little villages change hands on a barter system and despite my best efforts, I couldn't buy any of the plump tomatoes or green and red peppers that could be seen everywhere, peeking slyly out of back gardens.

Back at the boat I was surprised to be greeted in perfect English by the occupant of a kayak. Valetin came from Svistov and surprised me still further when he told me he was building a fourteen metre yacht there. Everything had to be made for it, the blocks, winches, brackets, bearings; like Zdenek and *Kondor* in Czechoslovakia and Andrei in Hungary, all the equipment was fashioned by Valetin or friends of his. He had designed the yacht himself and was building it in ferro-cement. He wanted to sail around the world and hoped to finish it in a year - if he has he should be sailing by now in *Kolombo Livia*, the *Concrete Stork*.

Valetin returned a little later, bearing a huge watermelon, a bucket of tomatoes and a bottle of Bulgarian red. He wanted nothing and I had by now run out of yachting magazines to give away. I offered to post some to him, but he was uncertain if they would arrive. Customs officials have a predilection for glossy western magazines when they check parcels coming into Bulgaria.

15th August   The approaches to Rousse are not encouraging. Chimneys belch out clouds of noxious gas and equally noxious looking effluent cascades into the river from the factories. So it's a bit of a surprise that the centre of Rousse is all Baroque buildings and little cafés and restaurants with the locals all out and about enjoying themselves despite the huge chemical factory on the Romanian side that sends clouds of chlorine laden fumes into downtown Rousse. We shop for everything we can get here because I know that in Romania there is little to buy in the shops.

16th August   I clear us out of Bulgaria in Rousse, but wait an hour before leaving until another of the violent storms which seem to be a feature of the lower Danube, has passed over. My abiding feeling for the country is that all my ideas of it have been turned inside out. Bulgaria is a bureaucratic country that can be difficult to travel in, but the effort is so often rewarded. Everywhere in Bulgaria I found an intense interest in *Rozinante's* trip down the Danube and a friendliness and generosity that turns many stereotypes of the country upside down - which just goes to show that you can't believe everything you read.

9 Romania

In Romania at Giurgiu opposite Rousse an armed guard is allotted to us and I begin the long process of clearing in. Unlike Rousse on the opposite shore, Giurgiu is not an attractive place, in fact the part of Giurgiu by the river is purely a river port surrounded by industry. The small town of Giurgiu is about two kilometres away, but it is mostly a dormitory suburb for the port and is a shabby, desperate place.

Romania is not used to small boats arriving on the river and the army, police, customs and immigration were all suspicious. When the harbourmaster starts shouting and waving at me, pushing the boat papers under my nose, the conscript translates for me that the harbourmaster is upset because the papers do not have my photo on them. They are no good. You cannot enter Romania.

I tell the conscript that they are normal British boat papers and he nods that he knows, but if I keep quiet and let the harbourmaster have his tantrum then after half an hour it will be all right.

Sure enough, after half an hour I get the papers stamped. In the customs office I sign a carnet which states that I am not carrying weapons, ammunition, radioactive materials, narcotics and psychotropic drugs, or prohibited records and books amongst other things. After a cursory search of the boat in which the well-stocked food lockers are admired, we eventually get permission to cruise the length of the Danube in Romania.

Our allotted armed guard, a young conscript studying forestry, guided me around the various offices. He fairly bubbled over being able to speak English and quizzed me on anything and everything, on the countries upstream, on England, on London, on the things you can buy in the shops, on *Rozinante* which he persisted in calling a 'playboat swimming in the river'. He turned out to be a friend indeed, whisking me through the various offices, constantly assuring me there was 'no problem' even when the officials shouted or pouted, interpreting my replies in the appropriate manner so that the army, police, customs and immigration were all satisfied. He had to do a twelve hour stint before he was relieved by another guard who watched over us through the night.

This procedure was to be repeated everywhere in Romania where a guard detail was ordered to watch over the diminutive *Rozinante* twenty-four hours a day. Mostly these young conscripts were amiable lads who would ask for 'souvenirs', Kent cigarettes which are an accepted form of barter, real coffee and magazines. I found out the young conscript in Giurgiu had studied forestry and gave him two *Scientific Americans* which he immediately buttoned inside his tunic, his face aglow with the anticipated pleasure of a foreign magazine.

Giurgiu is the closest place to make an excursion to Bucharest. If you arrive by cruise boat coaches are laid on, so I figured we should be able to hitch a lift to Bucharest on one of the cruise boat coaches. In the night two cruise boats had arrived with prearranged excursions to Bucharest the next day. In the morning the Romanian guide was willing, but the American courier was as stony faced and unrelenting as any Romanian bureaucrat. She insisted it was impossible to take us to Bucharest and it was only the intervention of the Romanian tour guide that got us on board.

Bucharest is often called the 'Paris of the East', but this reputation, gained between the two World Wars, was fast disappearing under President Ceausescu's plan to carpet the city in multi-storey apartment blocks and offices, a habitat he considered suitable for a truly socialist state even if it meant demolishing the old quarters, churches and cobbled squares, even the cathedral. Parts of the old city peep through the new, though so does the effect of a ruined economy: sewerage seeps into alleys, the roads are full of potholes, the electricity is turned off at ten o'clock plunging Bucharest and indeed Romania into darkness, the shop fronts are dressed but inside you will probably find you cannot buy any of the things in the window, in the bars and restaurants the menu is limited unless you can pay in hard currency. The fabric of what was once an elegant city is slowly crumbling. Despite all this there are glimpses that give you an idea of what Bucharest once was and of the almost unquenchable spirit of the Romanians themselves who still manage to enjoy life despite the hardships pressed on them from above.

Bucharest is a difficult place for the independent traveller to get around. Taxis are few and far between, the buses and trams are crammed to overflowing, and often you will arrive to find that what you want to see has just closed for lunch or for the rest of the day. For this reason if you have only a short amount of time in Bucharest I'd recommend a guided tour. I know, I know. Guided tours are not my cup of tea either, but I've toured Bucharest as part of a tour group and independently and the former is without doubt the easiest way to see the sights. Doing it independently means you will see more of the real Bucharest and be open to chance encounters with the inhabitants, but you can do that elsewhere as well. While looking around Bucharest independently I met a local who told me a typical self-deprecating joke about Bucharest and life under Ceausescu.

II *Rozinante*

A party member was granted permission to go to England for a conference and arrived in London where he wandered about the streets gazing in awe at the shop windows. He was even more astonished to find he could buy anything that was displayed in the shops, that goods of all kinds were freely available. When he returned to Bucharest he was asked about the trip. 'Well', he said, 'I went into a bakers and I could buy bread; I went into a tailors and I could buy a suit, any suit that I wanted; I went into a bookshop and I could buy books, there were hundreds of books all for sale; I could even buy any sort of car I wanted'. Mouths were agape amongst his fellow comrades until an old party cadre nodded sagely and said 'We were once like that you know ... but those English are twenty years behind the times'.

We had another little run-in with the American courier who must have been taking lessons from Ceausescu and refused to let us get on the bus.

We have to get back to the boat in Giurgiu.
Your problem. You are not entitled to travel on the coach. Find your own way back.

It took the kindly intervention of the Romanian tour guide to hustle us on board and get us back to the docks.

15th August I'm happy to leave Giurgiu where the sulphurous fumes from the industry nearby make it difficult to breathe, burning the lungs and making our eyes water. A sulphurous mist hangs over the river for ten kilometres downstream. We stop at Oltenita and wander ashore to a run-down restaurant and bar for a drink. A gypsy band is playing wild music with mixed success as they are obviously somewhat inebriated and the fiddle player keeps getting it wrong. Just as we get there a soldier runs up and orders us back on the boat. After an hour he has apparently radioed his superior who gives us permission to go ashore. The restaurant has run out of food, has no beer, the bottles of wine are $20 each, and the waiter wants a carton of cigarettes, so we go back to the boat for a cup of tea.

Later that night the harbourmaster invites us to his house for a drink. He speaks fluent French so Bridget translates the bits I miss. He wants to know all about the Rhine-Main-Danube Canal and is perplexed when I tell him it is not finished and probably won't be until 1993. He has heard that it is about to open in a month's time and has visions of all sorts of craft coming from the North Sea and stopping at Oltenita.

17th August   Cernavoda has to be one of the poorest places we have stopped at in Romania. I queued for half an hour for eggs, Bridget queued for another half an hour to get bread, there were hardly any vegetables to speak of had we bothered to queue, and the petrol station had been closed for days because it had run out of fuel and none was expected for a few more days. The whole town has a dusty forlorn look to it. Nearby a huge nuclear power station is being built to a Canadian design. Ceausescu criticised the amount of money it was costing and the amount of concrete being used - did orders come from the top to use less concrete? Will Cernavoda be added to the disaster list along with Chernobyl?

18th August   At Cernavoda a 60km long canal, the Danube-Black Sea Canal, considerably shortens the distance for cargoes to reach the Black Sea from the Danube. The alternative is another 300km along the winding channel of the Danube to the delta and Sulina. Work on this canal started in 1949 with what

II *Rozinante*

amounted to slave labour: peasants who resisted the collectivisation projects, minor criminals, critics of the party and anyone else who could be forced to work under whatever pretext. It is estimated that over a hundred thousand died during the initial construction until it was abandoned in 1953, earning it the title of the Canalul Mortii, the 'Canal of Death'. Ceausescu resurrected the canal project in 1973, though the route was changed to a more easterly direction so that the canal emerged to the south of Constanta at Agigea. Here a gigantic port has been built to accommodate what is hoped will be the large amount of traffic on the Danube when the Rhine-Main-Danube Canal is completed and it is possible to take a barge train of international proportions from the Black Sea to the North Sea. The canal was opened in 1984.

To transit the Danube-Black Sea Canal we must take a pilot, so in the morning Victor turns up, a cocky dark-haired man who immediately makes himself at home on the boat, changing into a pair of swimming trunks, smoking my cigarettes, putting tapes in the cassette player and then choosing a few cassettes for himself, fingering my jeans and examining my camera. When I explain it will take 10 hours or more for *Rozinante* to transit the canal he is aghast. Fortunately for us and for Victor he negotiates a tow alongside a barge in the lock and I forgive him for pocketing our tapes and smoking cigarettes like a train. As it turns out I won't thank him when he is gone.

Tied alongside *Rozinante* is doing 8 knots or more with the hull flexing and cracking under the strain. When the wind gets up on the nose water is sluiced up between the tug and *Rozinante* and in through the fitted windows. God only knows what it is doing to the hull and deck joint, distorted from the strain against the tugs side. There is not a lot we can do unless I cast

Rozinante off, so while Bridget mops up the water inside with towels, I'm pumping again.

There is little traffic on the canal. There is a lock at each end, though the distance we descended was less than a metre at the Cernavoda end and probably less than two metres at the Agigea end. When the Danube is high the descent down the locks will no doubt be considerably greater. Victor jumps off at the end of the canal with tapes, cigarettes and some coffee, but not my jeans which I tell him he can't have.

We potter through the huge commercial harbour at Agigea to the old harbour at Constanta. This new commercial harbour is vast and it takes a while to get to Constanta. Once we arrive we settle down for a cup of tea and then I figure we will have a look around Constanta. I cast around for my wallet in the boat and then start frantically searching under cushions and anywhere else I can think of. It had been sitting on a shelf in the saloon, but it isn't there now. It contains around $US400 and my credit cards. Fortunately Bridget has money so I borrow $US50 from her and set off to report the theft. I can't believe I have been so stupid.

I go to the army office in the harbour and try to explain my plight. The only result I get here is that they will come and check the boat in the evening at 2000. So I figure I need to get to the control tower and offices at the Agigea end of the canal where Victor left *Rozinante*. Finding a cab is next to impossible, but eventually a battered Dacia pulls up and the driver asks me where I want to go. I explain that I need to get to the offices at Agigea.

Twenty dollars. Contanta-Agigea-Constanta.

II Rozinante

This is way over the odds, but I figure I'm not in the best position to argue. I jump in the car and we are off to the canal offices. When we get there I don't pay the would-be cabby so I hope he won't go anywhere. I walk up to the offices and find a man in one of the downstairs offices. I don't get anywhere as he speaks no English or French and my Romanian is limited to pleasantries and bar-speak. He motions for me to wait and phones someone. In a few minutes a man in a suit arrives and asks me to go upstairs to another office. I enter a room with four men in suits. The one behind the desk asks me to sit down in perfect English and I breath a sigh of relief. At last someone who I can tell my tale of the theft of the wallet to.

All these guys seem big guys, dressed in black suits with well-fed features compared to your everyday Romanian like my 'taxi' driver.
What do you want here? Who brought you here?

I explain about *Rozinante*, my discovery of the loss of my wallet, and that I used a taxi to get here. He is not taking any notes.
But why did you come here? How do you know the man down there in the car? How did you meet him?

I explain again and then a slow realisation of my situation stirs in my neurons. These are Securitate, the feared secret police that Ceausescu uses to keep an iron grip on this country. I start working out how I am going to get out of this stuck in the middle of the port area. It's then I notice out of the window that three of these thugs are ripping my 'taxi' driver's Dacia apart. The seats have all been taken out. The boot is open and everything is out on the ground. The lining in the boot has been ripped out. The little five foot nothing driver is trying to stop

The Accidental Sailor

the six foot thugs who just shove him out of the way.
Who do you know in Romania? What is your work? Why are you here?

The guy behind the desk is relentless. After half an hour of this grilling I'm more than a bit worried. I ask him to take my details and make a report about the lost wallet. He scribbles a few details on a bit of paper, but I'm certain it will never leave his desk. A small plan has formed in my stunned brain. I've read somewhere that there is a power struggle between the army and the Securitate.

I have to meet the army commander in the port. I have an appointment at 2000.

They all look at each other when the guy behind the desk translates. I figure I have to take the initiative and pick up my jacket and indicate I will go back to the taxi. To my astonishment they tell me to go and I scuttle down the stairs and out the door to where my 'taxi' driver is still berating the heavies tearing his car apart.
Come on. Lets go.

I start putting seats and odd bits and pieces that lie scattered around the car back into it. The driver, still yelling like a banshee, gets the hint and puts the rest of his car back together. And we zoom off towards Constanta.
They are sheet. Securitate sheet.

He is hopping mad and I wonder about his sanity as he gesticulates back to the port offices and still somehow manages to keep his Dacia on the road.

II *Rozinante*

When we get back to Constanta I give him $US25. He needs it more than I do. And the army officer doesn't turn up to *Rozinante*, but I'm really past worrying. In fact I'm thankful to that army officer for his virtual presence in my meeting with the Securitate. Just happy to be back safe and sound on *Rozinante*. Even Bridget shows some sympathy for my close shave with the Securitate.

19th August   In Constanta we waited four days until a northeaster blew itself out. At times the gale was washing solid water right over the top of the breakwater which stands around 20ft high. Though we had any amount of Romanian lei, it was a struggle to find anything to spend it on. On one night I queued for over an hour at a pizza stall to get a couple for dinner. Eventually I arrived at the head of the queue and got the last two pizzas going. After that there were no more and yet the queue for the stall still stretched down the street. I will never forget the look on the face of the man behind me when it was announced that there were no more pizzas. There was a desperation about him, I almost thought he would burst into tears as he turned away. To my eternal shame I didn't give my two pizzas to him. I should have.

In Constanta harbour with us was a 25 foot wooden yacht with a Romanian flag. I had gone over to talk to him earlier, but had been warned not to do so by the army guard. Later in the evening he came over to *Rozinante* and invited us onto his yacht for a drink. I explained that we had been warned off by the guard and that he could get into hot water if we came on board.

Just come. Don't worry. My problem.

So we did. Inside Nicolas' neat little craft there was no boat furniture to speak of. We sat on scatter cushions on the cabin sole and he pulled a bottle of Bulgarian red out of a locker. His most treasured possession was an old brass compass. Like other boats in the communist countries along the Danube most of the gear on board had been fabricated by Nicolas or friends. He was ready to leave, but could not get the papers to do so.

It is impossible here. They guard the little sailing dinghies when they are training just outside the harbour. I cannot go out without a guard boat to escort me.

I mentioned I had seen the patrol boat out with the sailing dinghies when they are out training and racing. I guess when you are desperate a small sailing dinghy could be an escape vessel from the claws of Ceausescu's totalitarian state. Nicolas was getting maudlin with the wine and his situation locked into Romania.

Anyhow, one dark night I will just leave. I don't care about them. They have hurt me and my family enough already. I will just leave.

And somehow I hope he did.

Even with all our Romanian lei I could not get hold of petrol or diesel for the 200 mile trip across the Black Sea to the Bosphorus. We would have to do most of it under sail and just be patient about the trip. My plan was to go south down the coast towards the Bulgarian port of Burgas and if there were contrary winds, stop there to find fuel. If the winds were fair for Turkey and the Bosphorus, we would change course without stopping in Bulgaria.

10 The Black Sea

24th August   We left after the Romanian officials arrived at midday - they had said they would be there by eight in the morning. We left with the warning that we must proceed straight out to sea until we were ten miles off the coast before changing course for Bulgaria. We had a fair wind in the afternoon and through the night although the tubby little *Rozinante* was only making 3-4 knots under sail. She didn't come equipped with a big genoa, just the main and the working jib in plastic, but still we were happy to be under way and things are going smoothly enough.

We took three hour watches so that the person off-watch had just three hours to get some sleep. This system had worked well enough on *Roulette* and both of us were soon into the rhythm of a longer passage that should take around 2½ days at this speed. I was back to dead reckoning to get us down to the Bosphorus and Istanbul with just a chart, our estimation of speed and the compass bearing.

That night we had a celebration dinner of fried rice with the few vegetables we had been able to find and some leftover tins from the saloon locker. The water tank was full and I produced a bottle of Bulgarian red that had been stowed for the occasion.

In a light-hearted moment after the wine was finished I wrote a note saying who we were, where we were, and added my address in England for good measure before corking the bottle up and casting it over the side.

Over a year later a letter arrived in the post with a Bulgarian stamp on it. A couple walking on the beach had found the bottle with a message in it, but then had to find someone to translate the note inside. 'We are thinking of you in your little boat. If you come to Bulgaria please come to see us - you will be welcome'. It was a warming coda to the trip from Bulgaria.

25th August   *Rozinante* bounded on through the night and we had high hopes for a swift passage, well as swift as you can be in a Mirror Offshore 18 which is really not that swift at all. By the afternoon of our second day at sea we were off Burgas, but as the wind was fair for Turkey I decided not to enter Bulgaria and to continue on towards the Bosphorus. By the evening the wind had dropped and I was beginning to regret my rash decision. In Burgas I'm sure we could have found fuel and then we could fire up the outboard and make at least a couple of knots in the right direction instead of wallowing in the swell left over from the breeze.

As we sat in the cockpit after dinner I heard the low thrum of big diesels. In the hazy twilight it was difficult to make out the exact direction the noise was coming from. And then I spotted the grey outline of a large patrol boat idling along around half a mile off our port side. We sat there mesmerised while it passed and thanked our lucky stars that the patrol boat, likely Bulgarian, had not seen us. Then I heard the diesels approaching again and spotted the patrol boat coming back on a reciprocal course, but a bit closer to us. We watched it pass and then tried to catch the little wind that there was to get us on our way. Fat chance. I'm pretty sure they must have located us somehow, but perhaps because we were so small and the mast so short they couldn't get a good radar echo off us. For another two hours the diesels growled around us in the dark before the patrol boat finally pottered off elsewhere.

26th August   We wallow on towards the Bosphorus in a patchy breeze doing just a couple of knots when we are lucky. Still the dead reckoning plots are slowly dawdling towards the northern entrance to the Bosphorus.

In the afternoon we have a plague of flies that is like something out of the Bible. Hundreds of little flies arrive on board and buzz around everywhere. Fortunately they are not 'bitey' flies, but they are annoying, settling all over the boat and down below as well. And then like some Biblical deliverance two visitors arrive on board. Two diminutive fly-catchers land in the cockpit. They seem to have come from Turkey and be headed towards the Danube delta. In no time at all they are snapping up the plague of flies and they have a good appetite. I catch a couple of flies and hold them between my fingers for the flycatchers to take. There is just an imperceptible 'pick' as the birds pluck the flies from my fingers and then nimbly fly off to catch their own.

In the late afternoon one of the flycatchers departs, but the other one seems to have made himself at home on *Rozinante*. He sits on our hands, on my head, flies below and checks out the accommodation. By dusk the flies are gone, but our flycatcher is not done yet. He or she spies some giant moths migrating across the sea, moths that are almost as big as he/she is. Up the flycatcher goes and then there is the most amazing dogfight as the moth jinks and dives to avoid the bird. For at least 10 minutes the dogfight goes on like something out of World War II. Eventually the flycatcher wrestles the huge moth back to the boat and sits for a while getting its breath back while the moth flops about in the cockpit. And then this diminutive bird starts to eat this huge meal. And somehow finishes it. How will it take off again? But an hour later it heaves itself off the deck and sets off towards the Danube delta.

The whole show cheered us up no end and our slow progress under sail is all but forgotten. We are still headed in the right direction and we still have food and water.

27th August   My birthday. For my 38th year I decide we can postpone celebrations until we get to Istanbul since we have no alcohol left on board and we are down to eating tinned and dry goods. Not that I'm complaining. Romania was hardly a place to buy the makings of a birthday feast.

I know we are getting closer to the Bosphorus as the amount of shipping coming and going has increased and we need to keep a good lookout by day and night. There are fishing boats around as well, mostly the big Black Sea trawlers with top-heavy superstructures that often change course to come and take a look at us. I'm tempted to ask one of them for some fuel, but having come this far with just a dribble left in the tank I figure we can make it OK.

28th August   Around midday I am confident that we are near the entrance to the Bosphorus. I've been pretty blasé on the surface about my dead reckoning for the trip from Constanta, but for the last night and all of today I've had niggling doubts about it after four days at sea. I did use the trick of old and made my dead reckoning course slightly west of the entrance so that when I sight land I know I need to turn left a bit to find the entrance to the Bosphorus. There is tons, literally thousands of tons, of shipping around and a lot of local traffic as well. Once into the entrance I have just enough fuel left to crank the diesel up and get us into the Bosphorus against a rising head-wind.

Something over halfway down the Bosphorus is Bebek, a bight in the coast full of local yachts that wouldn't normally have a place for an average sized yacht. In *Rozinante* I squeeze into a gap and moor up. The local 'fixer' comes down to protest, but when I tell him we have just come from Romania he takes a long look at me, at *Rozinante*, at the sky, and then shakes his head and tells me it is 'no problem'. Thank you god, whoever you are, because I don't have any diesel left.

After Romania, Istanbul and Turkey seemed like a paradise, a land of plenty where you could buy food in the shops and dine on dishes in the restaurants that were unimaginable in Romania. On the day after we arrived I found Bridget had bought four loaves of bread during the day, a reflex action after Romania she said, in case it wasn't available tomorrow. We luxuriate in the comfort of this old city and both us have a certain glow at getting here in one piece.

11 Turkey

We spend a week indulging ourselves in Istanbul, almost believing we had arrived in the land of the lotus eaters. I had my postponed birthday feast in a wonderful fish restaurant in Bebek and drank far too much wine. It was as if we had thrown all pecuniary caution to the winds. Bridget bought a new dress and I bought a couple of new shirts. In down town Istanbul we indulged ourselves stopping in cafés on the slightest whim, eating simple but wonderful fish lunches and taking a taxi home every now and again.

What I did fail to do in Istanbul was find a stern gland fitting for *Rozinante*. I wasn't too worried by this figuring that the old one in there should last to Bodrum and in any case I intended to use the outboard for much of the time we might need to motor. My plan was to cross the Sea of Marmara down to the Dardanelles and then coast hop down the Turkish Aegean coast to Bodrum where I intended to leave *Rozinante*. The meltemi, the prevailing northerly wind should be behind us much of the time and more than strong enough to propel our small sail area swiftly along.

5th September   *Rozinante* has lots of goodies from the markets in Istanbul packed into her lockers and full tanks of petrol and diesel. It's time to go to Silivri along the northern coast of the Sea of Marmara. The meltemi is blowing on the quarter at 10-15 knots and we fly along the coast with one reef in the main and the jib. Things are a bit choppy and it takes us a little while to get back into boat fitness as *Rozinante* bobs and bounces along.

II *Rozinante*

By the time we get to Silivri we are both exhausted which has more to do with us than with the duration of the trip. Silivri is an odd place sporting a large prison and an odd little town. We wander ashore for a bite and then return to *Rozinante* for a long haul tomorrow down to Marmara Island not far off the northern entrance to the Dardanelles.

6th September   It's blowing strongly in the morning and I put the reef in the main and off we go. It's 45 miles to Port Marmara on the southwest corner of Marmara Island. This is a long old haul for us, but *Rozinante* is positively flying. By midday the wind is up and *Rozinante* is starting to broach. Those little shallow keels aren't keeping her in a straight line so it's time to take the main down altogether. We are out in the middle of the Marmara Sea now and going well with spray flying everywhere. The wind is up to 25 knots or so and this is the strongest wind that *Rozinante* has been in on the open sea. We hold on and surf around the corner of Marmara Island and into its lee. The wind is just as strong here, but there is protection from the swell and we dry off.

Port Marmara is a welcome refuge after a long day and we tie up near some of the big double-ended *mavis* that coast around the Black Sea carrying wheat, mixed cargoes and of course, marble. 'Marmara' is the Turkish for 'marble' and hence we get the Sea of Marble and Marble Island. The island is pock-marked with marble quarries which is not surprising since it has been quarried since antiquity. Greeks, Romans, Byzantines, Turks, all prized the silky white marble from here and shipped it all around their respective empires. We were rather more interested in the kebab shop than marble and indulged in beer, doner and pita bread.

7th September   It's nearly 60 miles to our next destination at Canakkale in the Dardanelles so we make a really early start. The meltemi is still whistling down from the northeast and we decide that the jib alone without any main will be adequate. So it is. *Rozinante* rockets along, well more accurately ploughs along, down to the entrance to the Dardanelles. There is shipping everywhere entering and leaving the Sea of Marmara via the narrow crack between Europe and Asia that opens onto the wide blue Aegean.

As we get closer to the Dardanelles the wind is accelerated down the narrow strait and we are a little out of control even with just the jib up. There is little we can do except try to stay in control as much as we can and avoid the shipping which is everywhere. We are pushed down into the neck of the Dardanelles as if some great weight is upon us that we can't do anything about. Firing up the diesel would be ineffectual and I don't think *Rozinante* will run straight and true under bare poles. The upside is that we must be doing a good 5 knots or more towards Canakkale.

By evening we zip around a corner in the Dardanelles where Canakkale sits in something of a bight and I fire up the diesel to head for the harbour. In the flatter water I get the jib down and we motor into the yacht basin looking a bit like a couple of drenched Argonauts. There are a couple of other yachts in here and bodies tumble onto the dock to help us tie up. The couple off the English 36 footer, a fine Westerly Conway, are full of questions.

What is the wind like? Have you come from just around the corner? Do you keep your boat here locally?
I explain that we have come from Port Marmara and that the

wind is pretty much as it is here. They have a whirling dervish of a wind generator on the back that does audibly make things sound a lot worse than it is. I can hardly hear myself speak above the whirr and whine of the windmill on the back of their boat. The couple disappear into their boat and then come out to talk to us again.

But where have you come from? Are you doing a mini-cruise around here?

I explain further.
We are on our way to Bodrum. We have come from Port Marmara today. Before that Istanbul and the Black Sea. We have come from England down the Danube.

They look at *Rozinante*. They look at us with some confusion. In this? From England in this?

I am getting a bit pissed at them calling my *Rozinante* a 'this'. Well if you will excuse us, we need a beer or two.

And I leave it at that and we wander off to the harbour café for a beer. Fancy calling the plucky *Rozinante* a 'this'.

8th September   In the morning we have a posse off the two boats quizzing us. Apart from the English couple on the Conway there is a sleek 42 foot Turkish yacht fully crewed up with half a dozen fit young Turks. They want to know if we are leaving and whether we think it is safe for them to leave. I'm bemused.

Listen, we will probably leave, but we are 18 foot long. You guys are much bigger. You should be fine.

The wind is blowing some 20 plus knots, but it is that whining wind generator that makes it all sound a lot worse than it is. We stow the boat and potter out with a wave to them all. Once out into the Dardanelles I hoist the jib and we zoom off down the strait. The others in the harbour are all out on the breakwater watching us, I guess to see what happens to us out there.

The Westerly Conway with the couple and their howling wind generator do leave and a few hours later have caught us. They have just a jib up as well. We wave and take pictures and they disappear off in front of us. The Turkish 42 footer is nowhere to be seen.

We are running a bit short on time if Bridget is to continue with me down to Bodrum. She has to get back to England and then points elsewhere on the globe, so I decide we will keep on going with this wind overnight and see where we get to for the next night. We run on down the Turkish coast until we get to the evocatively named Baba Burnu and turn the corner into a flat calm. No problem. We have petrol and I fire up the little outboard. We putter along at 3 knots, not quite the speeds we have been doing in the blustery meltemi, but progress in the right direction anyway. To the left of us are the towering mountains on the Turkish mainland and on the right the Greek island of Lesvos. Not until we get to the eastern corner of Lesvos do we pick up the wind again which now blows with renewed force from the east, not really the best direction to weather the island, but hopefully do-able.

We have dinner rounding the corner of Lesvos then Bridget goes off to get some sleep. The wind is up to 25-30 knots and I'm having real trouble controlling *Rozinante*. I decide I need to gybe and put the tiller over. Nothing happens. *Rozinante* just won't come round and we are headed for a group of rocks and

II Rozinante

reefs off the coast of Lesvos. I try again and again. Nothing. I figure I will need to fire up the diesel to help wear us around and give Bridget a call, a bit of a hysterical call as I watch the rocks getting nearer and nearer. Bridget comes up and I jump below to fire up. With the engine on quite high revs we manage to get her around and head away from the rocks. Panic over.

We storm on through the night until the wind begins to die down around six in the morning. I get the outboard out and start it up. We haven't gone very far before there is a bang at the back of the boat and while the outboard is still buzzing away, we aren't going anywhere. We must have hit something with the propeller and the shear pin has gone. No problem. I have a spare and hoist the outboard into the cockpit to do the repair while we bob around in a flat calm off the Karaburun Peninsula in Turkey. While I am getting the outboard prop off I notice a 40 foot motorboat with a large Turkish flag coming towards us. Aha, I think, good samaritans who have come to see if this little sailing boat needs any help. They get nearby and the captain walks out and leans over the side to talk to me.

Which one is Khios Island? I think it is that one.
He is pointing to Cesme Peninsula, a part of Turkey.
Not that one. It is further west.
I point to the hazy morning outline to the west.
Don't you have a chart?
No, no chart, not necessary.

I don't voice my thoughts on the matter, but I do tell him to be careful of the reefs in the northern approaches to Cesme. Somehow I'm not surprised when without further ado he goes back inside and accelerates away leaving us in a cloud of black diesel fumes. No, I tell a lie. I was a bit surprised.

I get the new shear pin in and put the outboard back on, fire it up, and away we go. By late morning there is a bit of wind again so I hoist the main and jib and we are sailing again. It might be a tubby little boat that looks like it has been modelled on a bath toy, but like any craft under sail there is magic to slipping along with just the wind to propel you. The shoosh of the water at the bows and the sizzle of water out back is soothing and so much more at one with the sea than the bone-shuddering diesel or buzzing outboard.

By afternoon we are around Cesme and sailing along the underbelly of the peninsula. There are a couple of deep bays along here and I figure that Kirkdilim towards the bottom will suit us. We sail up into it until headed by the wind and then use the outboard to get into the inlet at the head. Steep slopes drop down to turquoise water and we are the only ones here. With the anchor down we relax with a glass of wine while I cook up a Bolognese. We have covered what seems miles and really is quite a few miles and it's time to relax a bit before the final part of the voyage to Bodrum. We are nearly there.

10th September   We leave early in the morning and are soon bowling along under sail again heading for the strait between Samos Island and Turkey where just a mile separates the two countries. We whiz into the straits and are spat out the other side where a short distance away lies St Pauls Bay and the little cove of Ay Nicolaos. There is just a small Turkish fishing boat inside and we drop anchor in the shallows near the head of the bay. The wind is gusting off the hills, but with a draught of just 1.90 feet we can get close in to the shore.

We are just contemplating what to cook for dinner when the fisherman rows across with a plastic bag full of assorted fish.

We offer profuse thanks and then cook up a feast of fish and rice. And we still have a bit of wine left.

11th September   The next day is a relative hop-skip-and-jump to Gumusluk on the end of the Bodrum Peninsula. The meltemi is up again and with the reef in the main and the jib we fly across to Gumusluk. Our sturdy little ship is nearly home. We tie up on the jetty and go ashore for a celebratory meal in one of the restaurants here sitting at a table on the beach and watching the sunset.

Bridget has a few days left, though she needs to get to the comparative metropolis of Bodrum to arrange flights. I need to arrange for new credit cards to replace those stolen in Romania. It all seems so far away now here in the blue Aegean on the welcoming Turkish coast.

12th September   We potter the short distance around to Bodrum the next day. I see old friends and have one too many drinks with them. Without too much drama we have travelled down the Danube and across the Black Sea to the Mediterranean, possibly the furtherest a Mirror Offshore 18 has ever been. I can't say she is the most fleet sailing boat I have been on, nor the prettiest, but I do have a deep affection for her after this trip.

Bridget flies back to England and I organise for *Rozinante* to be hauled in a boatyard nearby and for repairs to be made to the stern gland. The repairs made in Czechoslovakia may have been a bit agricultural, but the repair has lasted for something over 1600 nautical miles so it all worked even if I did rest the diesel as much as possible. I put her up for sale with Murat the local broker, pack my notebooks and clothes and book a flight back to England.

12　Coda to the Danube Trip

My book on the Danube was published in 1991 (*The Danube: A River Guide*). A short time later a bizarre correspondence started when I got a letter from Tristan Jones. He was referring to a paragraph I had written in a section in the introduction summing up some of the travellers' accounts down the Danube over the last hundred years or more. Perhaps I was a little harsh, but I'll get on to that. What I wrote in the *The Danube* was:

John Marriner and September Tide made it up to Vienna where he wintered over in the Winterhafen. It is not until 20 years later that there is another account of a trip down the Danube, made by the irascible Tristan Jones in the same year I wandered down the river for the first time. Readers either adore or hate Tristan Jones' racy prose and pugnacious adventures. In *The Improbable Voyage* he recounts his voyage and his battles against German bureaucracy, a Czechoslovakian set-up (he believed) designed to wreck his boat, Bulgarian piracy and his single-handed attempts to reform Romania and free its people. You cannot deny the allure of the ripe tales, but there is a lot of fantasy mixed into the book and worse, a jingoism, a waving of the American flag, though he is Welsh, that has little to do with an understanding of eastern Europe and its peoples and promotes the sort of stereotypes that need to be dismantled rather than reinforced.

It wasn't long after that the publisher Imray received a letter from Tristan Jones. This is it verbatim (all capitals and underlining are his):

II Rozinante

CHIEF EDITOR   DANUBE

SIR
I'VE BEEN ASKED TO REVIEW 'THE DANUBE' (HEIKELL) FOR MAGAZINES. I'VE WRITTEN THAT FOR THE SKIPPER OF ANY SMALL CRAFT ON THAT RIVER IT'S NEXT TO USELESS. ON THE COVER BLURB IT SAYS IT'S A 'KILOMETER BY KILOMETER GUIDE FOR USE BY NAVIGATORS'. THAT'S UNTRUE. THE ONLY TWO GOOD GUIDES ARE THE SET OF CHARTS FROM THE DANUBE COMMISSION AND MY OWN 'DANUBE PILOT'. OF THE TWO THE LATTER IS BY FAR THE BEST, AS IT'S IN ENGLISH, FRENCH & GERMAN. DEPTHS (MIDDLE) BRIDGE- HEIGHTS, WIDTHS – AND 32 BITS OF NECESSARY INFORMATION FOR EVERY POSSIBLE HAVEN ARE GIVEN FOR THE WHOLE LENGTH OF THE DANUBE FROM INGOLSTADT TO THE BLACK SEA. LAST YEAR, WHILST SERVING AS COMMODORE OF CONSTANTA MARINA AND THE ROMANIAN DANUBE, I BROUGHT IT UP TO DATE. WOULD YOU CARE TO SEE SAMPLE PAGES?
YOURS SINCERELY
TRISTAN JONES   FRGS, FR INST.NAV, AUTHOR 17 BOOKS, HOLDER JOHN MORGAN PRIZE 1990.
PS. HEIKELL DESPITE HIS ANTI-TRISTAN-ISM HAS NEVER MET ME. I WONDER IF IT WAS BECAUSE HE KNEW I'D ... (text lost)

Appended to the back was another letter:

Rod Heikell c/o I,L,N & Wilson

I want to know <u>why</u> you stated in your 'The Danube' words to the effect that I <u>lied</u> or <u>exaggerated</u> in <u>'The Improbable Voyage'</u>. I want <u>details</u>.
Every step of my voyage was <u>witnessed</u> and much documented. It's <u>all true</u>.
I want an apology from you published in 'Navigation News', Motorboat & Yachting and 'Yachting World'. I want you to say you'll do this ASAP. Or I take legal action, and, on advice take you to court and demand maximum recompense.
Tristan Jones

Now this letter shook me up a bit. Well quite a lot really. The publishers suggested the matter could be debated in the yachting magazines. I decided to send a letter of apology first. I quote parts of it here because it was quite long.

Dear Tristan Jones
For a paragraph in an inconsequential book on the Danube which will probably only sell a few thousand if I'm lucky you seem to have developed an intense hatred of me. Why? We've never met so you don't have any idea of me apart from a few hints here and there in *The Danube*. We've never corresponded apart from your reply to a letter circulated around the yachting magazines and to which I briefly replied. I think you take me too seriously as a threat to your name and your books. I think you take me more seriously than I do.
So what in the end is the problem? That I criticized *The Improbable Voyage*? Yes I did and I stand by what I said. Well

mostly. I felt that the book wasn't one of your best - certainly not as good as *The Incredible Voyage* or *Saga of a Wayward Sailor* or *A Steady Trade*. Oh yes I've read them and I even remember some articles in *Seahorse* from before *The Incredible Voyage* was published. I like the books and have always said so, but it doesn't mean that I have to be blind to things I didn't like and considered erroneous in *The Improbable Voyage*.

If I was critical about Lake Titicaca or the Amazon where I have not sailed then fair cop - call me names and tell me to piss off - but don't do it for those places I visited on the Danube. I'm not some armchair bound critic sounding off about things I haven't experienced or seen. ...

So what is the problem here? If I hurt you with my paragraph then I apologise for that. I wouldn't have written it if I had thought it so wounding. But are you really going to tell me it's such a big issue if I turn up and ask you. I don't think most people care a jot about the paragraph and I am certain it doesn't diminish your standing anywhere...

One last thing and for this I'll apologise for just about anything. [Tristan Jones was sailing his trimaran to raise awareness of young adults with a disability and intended to use it to show that the disabled could carry out sea voyages as well as able bodied adults.] I grew up with a brother in a wheelchair (polio then muscular dystrophy) in a single parent family.

This is not a sob story. I know what life is like for the handicapped and the handicaps the rest of the population have in dealing with someone with a disability, in my brother's case principally that they assume a person is somehow mentally deficient because he is physically handicapped. He died when he was 18 and I wish he could have seen some of the world that I subsequently have travelled through. So anyone who

does anything for the handicapped gets my plaudit - whether you like it or not...
Rod Heikell

There followed further letters getting somewhat more bizarre. Tristan Jones didn't want to debate the matter in a yachting magazine. In one he wrote 'First you boast of your 'fighting alone'; next you'll contact the yachting magazine of my choice ... You really should make up whatever mind you have.' Next to this was written in pen 'The One True God judges'. The threats to take me to court for all I had and the offer to Imray of his own 'Danube Pilot' because my 'bodge-up' would cause 'a bad accident' or even cause someone to 'die' continued. He never did send his own pilot to Imray. But things were to get even more bizarre with subsequent correspondence.

TRISTAN JONES, THE ANCHORAGE , RAWAI, THAILAND
March 8th ninety-two
Mr W G Wilson ,
''The Danube ''
Sir
I've just waded through the above turgidity again.

As you have not seen fit to communicate with me on my complaints about Heikell's book nor to make any mention of apology or explanation, I am going to publish and keep publishing - but not where it will cause sales of 'The Danube' - the following statement until you inform me what's been positively done about Heikell's libelling my book 'The Improbable Voyage':

Rod Heikell's book 'The Danube' is plagiaristic, full of errors and will certainly place in jeopardy the vessel of any voyager using it for reference in navigation of the River

Danube. In future, until I get satisfactory word back from either Heikell or his publisher, I shall refer to him as 'Butch'. Certain mannerisms in the way he writes about his women companions - plus his first name - lead me to suspect that, besides being fascist, Heikell is a lesbian. Reliable witnesses have told me that Ms Heikell emptied her toilet-bucket straight into the Danube all the way downstream, and that both her companions looked like KGB drivers in drag. Imray, Laurie, Noray and Wilson Ltd is in this case an irresponsible publisher which seems not ...*(and here follows the usual list of grievances about lies, exaggeration, irresponsibility, etc.*
Truly
Tristan Jones
Copies to appropriate professional organizations, authorities and agents. Copy to be appended to my Will and Testament.

There were a few other letters and a copy of an article he wrote for *The Salisbury Review*, a conservative quarterly expressing far right views. Tristan Jones article was entitled *Splendid Remembrances: Tristan Jones sails down the Red Danube* where he complains about the villainous UK press and me (again):

But for 'The Improbable Voyage' there were hardly any notices in the UK press. A couple of critics snarled that I had been 'looking for trouble so I could write about it'. Later, Rod Heikell, a 'yacht-guide' hack, who'd been wafted down the Danube in Soviet ferries in '85, and who obviously doesn't know his Marx from Donald Duck, wrote that I had exaggerated the obstacles on my Danube voyage and that I had been provocative, by for instance wearing my boat's national ensign and my own flag through five communist countries (on an international waterway). I wonder: did these poor wretches never know the joy of cocking a snook at bullies from the safety of their father's shadow...

Correspondence dried up after this, but I figured that on a voyage planned for 1995 to SE Asia that I would go and talk to him there. Somehow I imagined a fairly robust conversation with a drink together at the end of it. It was not to be. Tristan Jones died in June 1995. Over a decade later the author Anthony Dalton got in touch with me. He was writing a biography of Tristan Jones and was curious about the correspondence on the Danube.

We met and over coffee it turned out that the truth was even more bizarre than the correspondence suggested. Tristan Jones' books were a curious mix of fact and fiction as was his life story. The biography Anthony Dalton wrote, *Wayward Sailor: In Search of the Real Tristan Jones,* makes for a fascinating read, at least it did for me after the foregoing correspondence. And there is much not mentioned in the biography. And no, I'm not actually a lesbian.

Rozinante was eventually sold to an American living in Izmir and working for NATO. Alvis wanted the boat to potter around the Gulf of Izmir and though I have kept an eye out for *Rozinante* when I have been in the vicinity, sadly I have not seen the brave little boat again.

II *Rozinante*

Mirror Offshore 18

MK I

Barge train on the Danube

Rozinante parked up in South London with the trusty Rover

Rozinante hauled out in Czechoslaovakia with the Pharoah and the Bulgar carrying out repairs

The Accidental Sailor

Zdenek's *Kondor* in Bratislava

Rozinante nudged into the bank in Yugoslavia

Flycatcher visitor on the Black Sea

Bridget spruces *Rozinante* up

Rozinante alongside the tug in the Danube-Black Sea Canal